Friendly Guides to Technology

A Friendly Guide to Developer Advocacy

Everything You Need to Know to Become a Developer Advocate and Crush Your First 90 Days

Linda Ikechukwu

Apress®

A Friendly Guide to Developer Advocacy: Everything You Need to Know to Become a Developer Advocate and Crush Your First 90 Days

Linda Ikechukwu
Lagos, Nigeria

ISBN-13 (pbk): 979-8-8688-2461-6 ISBN-13 (electronic): 979-8-8688-2462-3
https://doi.org/10.1007/979-8-8688-2462-3

Managing Director, Apress Media LLC: Welmoed Spahr
Acquisitions Editor: Anandadeep Roy
Project Manager: Jessica Vakili

Cover designed by eStudioCalamar

Distributed to the book trade worldwide by Springer Science+Business Media New York, 1 New York Plaza, New York, NY 10004. Phone 1-800-SPRINGER, fax (201) 348-4505, e-mail orders-ny@ springer-sbm.com, or visit www.springeronline.com. Apress Media, LLC is a Delaware LLC and the sole member (owner) is Springer Science + Business Media Finance Inc (SSBM Finance Inc). SSBM Finance Inc is a **Delaware** corporation.

For information on translations, please e-mail booktranslations@springernature.com; for reprint, paperback, or audio rights, please e-mail bookpermissions@springernature.com.

Apress titles may be purchased in bulk for academic, corporate, or promotional use. eBook versions and licenses are also available for most titles. For more information, reference our Print and eBook Bulk Sales web page at http://www.apress.com/bulk-sales.

Any source code or other supplementary material referenced by the author in this book is available to readers on GitHub. For more detailed information, please visit https://www.apress. com/gp/services/source-code.

If disposing of this product, please recycle the paper

To me, myself, and I, for constantly daring to dream beyond the limits of my background.

Table of Contents

About the Author

Linda Ikechukwu is an experienced developer education professional. She began her career as a software engineer, working across cloud engineering, front-end development, and cybersecurity. This breadth of experience gave her firsthand insight into how developers evaluate tools, learn new systems, and adopt technology in real-world environments.

She has led and shaped developer education strategies at some of Silicon Valley's most disruptive startups, creating practical programs that help teams lower the learning curve for complex tools and drive real adoption. Her work has earned her a global technical writing award, and she has delivered keynotes and talks at over 40 conferences across four continents.

She wrote this book for developer advocates, educators, technical leaders, and anyone tasked with driving adoption of technical products but rarely taught how to do it well. It offers the playbook she wished existed earlier in her career, bridging the gap between shipping great technology and helping developers actually succeed with it.

When she's not writing, speaking, or teaching, Linda can be found traveling the world, moonlighting as a travel influencer, or on a tennis court. You can learn more about her at lindaikechukwu.com.

About the Technical Reviewer

Sam Julien is a developer relations leader and product manager who has built and scaled developer programs and products at Auth0, Okta, and WRITER. He's also the author of *Getting Started in Developer Relations*, the *Developer Microskills* newsletter, and *Agentic Graph RAG*. Sam's favorite thing in the world is spending time in the beautiful Pacific Northwest with his family. You can find more of his work at samjulien.com.

Acknowledgments

Huge thanks to Gift Egwuenu, Ruth Ikegah, Edidiong Asikpo, and Olayinka Oshidipe for contributing their knowledge to sections of this book. Your work deserves global recognition. Nigeria to the world.

A special thank-you to Sam. You have never met me, yet you continue to support and cheer me on. My career in developer relations would not be the same without you. Thank you for agreeing to review this book.

Introduction

Unlike programming, there are no degrees or formal courses for developer advocacy. Most people enter this field by chance, learning on the job, making countless mistakes, and facing numerous uncertainties. The role isn't as clearly defined as other tech careers, which often leaves developer advocates struggling to figure out the right path on their own.

This was also my experience.

My name is Linda Ikechukwu, and I am a technologist with over eight years of experience in roles ranging from Cloud Engineering to Front-End Engineering and now Developer Advocacy. When I was first hired as a developer advocate, guidance was sparse, inconsistent, and often unclear. I had to figure out everything from scratch—how to succeed in my role, build a Developer Advocacy program, and earn a promotion.

This book is the guide I wish I had. It is for anyone who wants a structured path to succeed in developer advocacy, avoid common mistakes, and build a thriving career.

This book is for you if you are

- **An aspiring developer advocate:** You will learn how to move from curiosity to getting your first role. You'll pick up the skills you need to transition successfully, build a strong portfolio, create a compelling resume, navigate interviews, and make yourself an attractive hire for companies.

- **A newly hired developer advocate:** You will gain a robust understanding of the role, learn how to start strong, level up quickly, and become a trusted voice within your company and community. You'll also develop a strategy for contributing value from your first 90 days onward.

- **A working developer advocate:** You will fill gaps in your understanding, gain fresh insights, and have tools to share with your team or onboard new hires faster.

What can you expect from this book?

It begins at the foundation, helping you understand what a developer advocate actually does. From there, it guides you on how to get hired, covering everything from building a portfolio and resume to spotting red flags in interviews and excelling in the hiring process.

It also serves as a companion for your first 90 days on the job. You will learn how to settle in smoothly, clarify expectations, build key relationships, and understand your product, company, and community so you can make a real impact. You will also discover systems for maximum productivity using AI tools and practical advice for executing your role effectively.

A large part of the book focuses on content, because content is a central part of a developer advocate's job. Every edition of the State of DevRel Survey shows that individual contributors spend most of their time on content development. A review of over 100 developer advocacy job postings on startup.com confirms this. Every listing includes technical content creation as a core responsibility, often described as "creating awareness, guiding, educating, and engaging developers through blogs, webinars, tutorials, code examples, and presentations." If you want to succeed in this role, mastering content is not optional, it is essential.

To provide a broader view, some chapters include contributions from accomplished developer relations professionals. Their insights and experiences offer practical lessons drawn from multiple voices, giving you guidance beyond my own.

Why struggle to figure it all out on your own when you can follow a proven framework, help developers succeed, and grow your career at the same time?

PART I

Introduction to Developer Advocacy

When you talk about becoming a Developer, getting into DevOps, or simply writing code, it's relatively straightforward to grasp what the job entails, as these fields are well-established and widely understood. They come with clear expectations and structures, thanks to their popularity in the market. However, Developer Advocacy is a newer and less conventional field, often leading to misconceptions about what the role actually involves.

That's why it would be a disservice if I didn't start this book by clarifying what Developer Advocacy truly is, and what it is not. This section of the book clears up those misconceptions, offering a detailed look at Developer Advocacy as both a field and a job role.

Oftentimes, when I tell people my job title, the first question I get is *"Advocate? Are you a lawyer?,"* which is slightly hilarious.

If you're planning to become a Developer Advocate, it's essential to first understand what the role is all about, don't you think? That's what we discuss in these chapter.

CHAPTER 1

What Is Developer Advocacy?

The Merriam-Webster English dictionary defines advocacy as *the act of publicly speaking up for, supporting or representing a cause, policy or group of people.*

Developer advocacy as a professional role closely mirrors the dictionary definition of advocacy. It involves publicly representing and promoting a technical product or tool to developer audiences. The goal is to build relationships with developers, raise awareness of the tool and its benefits, and equip them with the information and training they need to successfully adopt it. In doing so, developer advocates directly contribute to driving company goals..

If you've done any prior research on developer advocacy, then you must have come across the term ***developer relations***. The difference between developer relations and developer advocacy is often an early point of confusion for new entrants.

Developer Relations (DevRel) is the summation of all the professional activities that go into the practice of engaging with developers as the primary users and influencers on purchases of a product on their journey with the said product and said company.

To better understand the role and importance of developer advocacy, we must discuss developer relations.

© Linda Ikechukwu 2026

L. Ikechukwu, *A Friendly Guide to Developer Advocacy*, Friendly Guides to Technology, https://doi.org/10.1007/979-8-8688-2462-3_1

1.1 The Rise and Importance of DevRel Practitioners

In 2011, Marc Andreessen famously declared that software will eat the world, and it surely has. Everywhere you turn, there's a software product or app for almost every use case.

The rise of SaaS (Software as a Service) transformed the software purchase model, giving individual developers more influence over the tools they chose to use. Additionally, as IT skills became more accessible and democratized, the software developer workforce grew significantly. Both trends led to the emergence of numerous businesses focused on creating tools, products, and APIs to help developers build software more efficiently and easily.

In turn, with developers becoming crucial decision-makers and a route to market, the practice of Developer Relations—which had existed since Apple pioneered Developer Evangelism in the 1980s—found new relevance and urgency.

Technology adoption doesn't happen in isolation. These Devtool companies soon realized that having dozens of engineers with top-notch technical skills wasn't enough to distinguish their product in a competitive market. They realized they needed people who would dedicate their time to developing strategies to increase product visibility, educating the community and supporting them through experimenting, prototyping, and building, which hopefully leads to them releasing something into production. However, since developers are naturally discerning consumers, conventional marketing approaches weren't effective.

The solution was to hire DevRel professionals—individuals who possess a strong technical foundation, an understanding of the developer mindset, and the communication prowess and creativity required to actively engage with and influence tech communities.

This led to the popularity of DevRel Practitioners.

1.2 Components of Developer Relations

DevRel is everything that's done to ensure that a product's target developer community can move from discovery to adoption as quickly and frictionlessly as possible. It does this by optimizing developer touchpoints (as shown in Figure 1-1), that is, those interactions that map a developer's experience along the way, to increase product adoption and revenue potential.

It is an umbrella term for all the activities needed to ensure a developer finds success with your product.

Scenario: A developer searches *"How to do masked phone numbers for anonymous call pairing"* on Google. Everything they interact with (how they engage, what and whom they engage with, how it makes them feel, and how they react) to go from discovering that Twillo can solve this particular problem for them, learning how they can possibly integrate Twilio into their ecosystem, to building a solution with Twilio on production, and maintaining that solution falls under DevRel.

Developer Journey Map

	DISCOVER	EVALUATE	LEARN	BUILD	SCALE
GOALS/ NEEDS	*Is this of use to me?*	*Will it meet my needs?*	*How does it work?*	*Can I build a proof of concept?*	*Can I build to scale?*
QUESTIONS	1. What is it? 2. Could it solve my problem? 3. Is it credible?	1. Does it look easy to use? 2. Are there any red flags? 3. Is pricing a barrier?	1. Time to 'Hello World' 2. Are the Docs a good experience? 3. Do I have confidence? 4. Is there a community?	1. Speed to MVP 2. Is the product a good experience? 3. How do I get support? 4. Is it value for money?	1. Can I do more? 2. How do I give feedback? 3. How can I contribute? 4. Will the product grow with me?
INTERNAL TOUCHPOINTS	Dev Hub Landing Page SEO / PPC Social Events Blog Newsletter Case Studies	**DEVELOPER EXPERIENCE: PRODUCT + DOCS** Docs Landing Page FAQs Product pages Forums Use Cases Pricing Page Webinars	Getting Started / Quick Start Guide Code Samples Tutorials Sign up / Registration Office Hours Training Learning Resources	Extensions Sandbox Reference Guide Changelog Support Workshops	Developer Success SLAs Product Roadmap Showcase Ambassador Program Partner Program Certification
EXTERNAL TOUCHPOINTS	Online Media / Press Syndication Events, Meetups, Hackathons Referrals Online & Offline Groups	GitHub Stack Overflow	Technology Dependencies		

***Figure 1-1.** Developer Journey Map, showing the life cycle of a developer's relationship with a product. Each stage—Discover, Evaluate, Learn, Build, and Scale—includes common questions, needs, and touchpoints that DevRel teams can influence to drive adoption and retention. Originally created by Caroline Lewko and James Parton*

As Figure 1-1 illustrates, guiding a developer from discovery to scale is no small feat. It involves a range of activities, which we will explore next.

Depending on the company, developer advocates may undertake all or some of the activity categories relating to the internal or external touchpoints as part of their responsibilities.

These are as follows.

1.2.1 Developer Experience

Developer Experience (DX) is the equivalent of User Experience, where the user in this case is a developer. Developer Experience makes sure that developers are able to easily adopt a product or set of technologies into their existing infrastructure or technology stack. Functionally, DX sits with Product, Engineering, or the CTO's office, depending on the company size.

In some companies, you would find the role Developer Experience Engineer, a core software engineer dedicated to enhancing the productivity, satisfaction, and success of developers using a company's products. Their job would usually be to develop and maintain extension tools and platforms that enhance developer productivity with a product like APIs, SDKs, custom command-line interfaces, code generators, integrations, debugging tools, etc. It may also fall on the DX engineer to maintain the necessary documentation of these productivity tools.

1.2.2 Developer Education

Developer Education (DevEd) involves creating, managing, and delivering educational resources (content) and programs in a variety of formats designed to help a company's target developers learn new skills, understand complex technologies or processes in order to effectively use a product. These educational resources are critical to the adoption and effective use of developer products. If developers cannot figure out what's possible with a product or if it can apply to their environment peculiarities, adoption is unlikely to happen.

1.2.3 Developer Marketing

Developer marketing—otherwise known as B2D or business to developer marketing—is marketing specialized for software developer audiences because Developers are a different kind of audience from mainstream end users. These character differences impact messaging, channels, tone of voice, tactical mix, and pretty much everything else that a marketer who markets to developers might do. They are a set of outreach activities designed to create awareness as developers discover and evaluate a product.

1.2.4 Developer Success

Developer Success provides support to developers as they go from evaluating a product to building a full-blown commercially scaled product. They help unblock and support community participants, prospects, or customers to foster and strengthen relationships and trust, which leads to better **retention** and use of the product. They also encourage **engagement** with the end users and champions who leverage their products to solve real challenges.

1.2.5 Developer Community

The summation of DevRel activities is community enablement. "Community" includes a company's employees (at the very least, the relevant product division), current customers, as well as prospects, and anyone who could in the future be interested in using the product... which is a fairly broad group of people. Granted enablement is a novel endeavor, and it takes place in some shape or form across teams. Developer Relations just makes it better suited to the developer technical audience. DevRel involves a variety of roles and activities that collectively work to engage, support, and grow this community.

1.3 The Place of DevRel Within a Company

While every company that views developers as a route to market must adopt developer relations (DevRel) as a company-wide culture, organizations quickly realize the need for a dedicated team to champion these efforts.

Within companies, the role of developer advocacy is a crucial part of and falls under the broader practice (and department) known as DevRel. The rest of the team may be made up of roles whose responsibilities move the needle across the core pillars of Developer Experience, Developer Education, Developer Marketing, and Developer Success. These roles often include Developer Experience Engineers, Developer Advocates, Community Managers, Technical Writers, or Developer Marketers. Together, they help developers discover, learn, and succeed with a product.

For example, the GitLab Developer Relations team that is under Marketing (1) is made up of

- Contributor Success Engineers who ensure that individuals who want to contribute code to Github can do so successfully. Their responsibilities include improving the Gitlab contribution process, responding to and triaging community issues, reviewing and merging requests, and providing guidance to community contributors on both technical and non-technical aspects.

- Community Program Managers who support communities by fostering mutually beneficial relationships between our program members and GitLab. They also track the communities' preferred methods of using GitLab and translate this knowledge into insights that help GitLab create a better product.

- Developer Advocates who support and grow GitLab's user community. They engage with GitLab community members through deep technical content, such as blog posts, demos, videos, contributed articles, podcasts, and social media. They also facilitate targeted programs and events. Their content and engagement efforts inspire a community centered around GitLab and drive our strategy to increase awareness, adoption, and contribution to GitLab.

Depending on the structure of the company, the stage the company is at, or what its business model is, the DevRel may fall under the bigger Marketing, Product, or Engineering team and may prioritize some pillars over others.

Small (< 201) and Medium (201–1000) companies most frequently have 2–5 employees in their DevRel teams, under 5000 people in their developer communities, and report to Marketing, while Large (1001+) companies most often have 11–25 employees in their DevRel teams, report to Product and boast over 2 million members in their developer communities.

Source: https://www.stateofdeveloperrelations. com/2023devrelreport

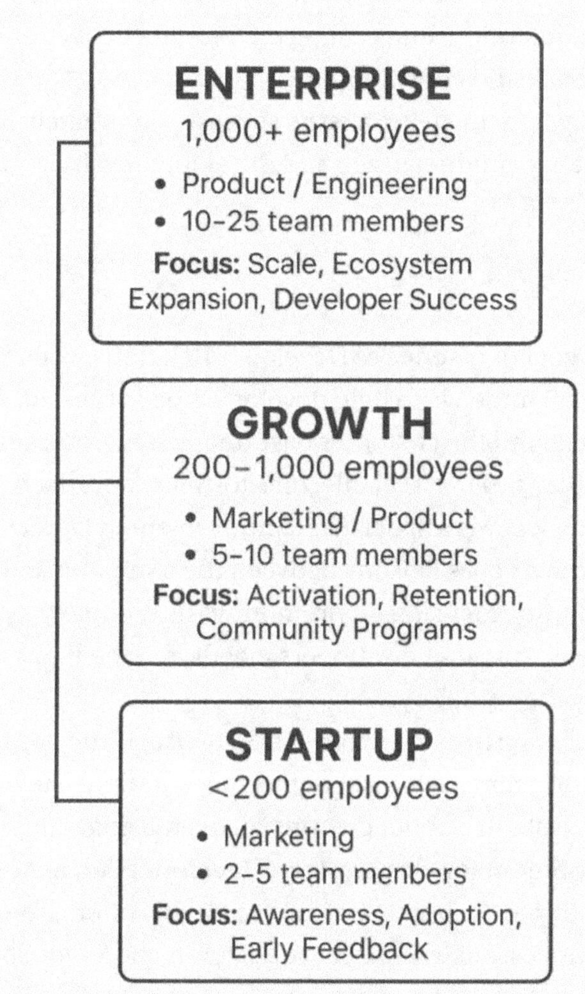

Figure 1-2. *How DevRel evolves across company stages*

As illustrated in Figure 1-2, this difference in structure reflects the company's immediate need. In early commercial days, DevRel often falls under Marketing because the priority is generating awareness and driving initial usage. As a company matures, DevRel often shifts to

Product or Engineering because the priority changes from acquisition to deep adoption, retention, and scaling the product ecosystem through community feedback and contributions.

Regardless of where the team sits, its success is ultimately measured by its ability to influence product usage and developer loyalty.

Summary

In summary, the goal or essence of Developer Relations, which developer advocacy efforts fall under, is to help developers be successful with a product so as to expand the customer base and achieve corporate goals (whatever those may be) in a scalable, one-to-many approach.

Developer Advocacy is a specialized multi-talented DevRel role. Developer Advocates act as liaisons between the company and the developer community, focusing on promoting the company's products to developers and ensuring that developers' needs and feedback are heard and addressed by the company.

Imagine it this way. In a large tech expo, **DevRel** is the entire expo, including all the different sections: booths, presentations, networking events, and help desks. It's about creating an overall engaging and supportive environment for all attendees. **Developer Advocacy,** on the other hand, is one specific booth at the expo. At this booth, representatives engage with attendees, answer specific questions, gather feedback, provide demos, and ensure that the feedback is relayed back to the company to improve products.

Links

1) https://handbook.gitlab.com/handbook/
    marketing/developer-relations/

CHAPTER 2

What Does a Developer Advocate Do?

Chapter 1 explored what developer advocacy is and how it fits into the broader world of developer relations. Now it's time to get more concrete: what does a Developer Advocate actually do once they're hired? What skills do employers look for, and what does the day-to-day work really involve?

The short answer is, a lot. Developer advocacy is a multi-faceted role that touches product, engineering, marketing, sales, and community—all through the lens of helping developers succeed. Depending on the company, you may find yourself writing docs, building prototypes, giving talks, designing workshops, or gathering feedback. The mix changes, but the mission stays the same: drive awareness and adoption by educating, empowering, and listening to developers.

But as exciting as that sounds, the role isn't for everyone. Developer Advocacy is highly public, demands comfort with ambiguity, and requires constant context switching. You'll juggle code, content, and community while often carving out your own career path in a field that's still young and sometimes misunderstood. This chapter unpacks both sides: the skills and activities that define the role, and the challenges that might make you pause before deciding it's the right path for you.

L. Ikechukwu, *A Friendly Guide to Developer Advocacy*, Friendly Guides to Technology, https://doi.org/10.1007/979-8-8688-2462-3_2

2.1 Developer Advocates Are Technical Jacks of Many Trades

The role of a developer advocate is to drive adoption and awareness of a technical product. This is primarily achieved through education and supporting developers as they navigate through the key touchpoints of the developer journey map: discovery, evaluation, learning, building, scaling, and referring fellow developers to the product.

When it comes to **how** to drive adoption and awareness, several activities expected of developer advocates can move the needle for developers at various stages of their journey, such as

- Writing documentation (**evaluate, learn**)

- Library development (**adoption, evaluate, build, scale**)

- Quick start apps (**adoption, build**)

- Blog posts (**awareness, discover, learn**)

- Webinars (**awareness, discover, learn**)

- Event sponsorship and Conference booth (**awareness**)

- Talks (**awareness, acquisition**)

- Support on developer forums like Stack Overflow (**activation, retention, product**)

- Pre-sales technical discussions via calls, emails, or support (**acquisition, activation**)

- Design and delivery of sales enablement training (**evaluate, acquisition, activation**)

- Dedicated community programs (**awareness, pipeline, retention**)

- Office Hours (**activation**, **retention**)

- Capture developer feedback (**retention, product**)

As you can see, the scope is broad and the possibilities are endless. However, ultimately, the activities you focus on depend on the company's strengths and weaknesses, the needs of your developer audience, and your own abilities.

Because the role overlaps with product, engineering, marketing, sales, and community, advocates often step in to bridge gaps where they exist. That is why the role is so often misunderstood: it looks different from company to company.

At Company A, the need might be deeply technical, such as building SDKs, improving docs, or smoothing the developer experience. At Company B, the need might be more outward-facing, such as content creation, community engagement, and storytelling. As an advocate, you cannot do everything at once, so you have to balance three questions:

- What does the company need most right now?

- What do developers need most from you?

- Where do your strengths lie?

You need to balance all three to be an effective developer advocate. And, you don't have to fill all the gaps all at once.

2.2 Developer Advocates Code, Create Content, and Engage the Community

"We look for people that have solid technical and communication skills, but also have experience engaging with the community and/or creating high-quality technical content."

~*Omar Sanseviero, **Head of Platform and Community at HuggingFace on WrittenCast Episode 2 (1)**

A day in the life of a developer advocate may look something like this:

- Writing documentation? Check.

- Producing tutorials and how to guide? Yep.

- Building prototypes and finding flaws in your onboarding flow? Naturally.

- Attending events, either just to interact with the attendees or to speak? (Mic) Check.

- Engage the community by answering questions on StackOverflow or Reddit? Upvote.

- Explore how to use the product in different domains, and much more.

While the specifics vary, most advocacy work falls into the three interconnected pillars of code, content, and community.

2.2.1 Code (Technical Background)

As a developer advocate, one of the questions I get asked a lot by intending developer advocates is: "Do I need to be technical to become a developer advocate?". My answer is Yes.

In the 2023 State of Developer Relations Survey (2), 77% of DevRel practitioners reported having some form of formal technical education or training in technology, engineering, or computer science. Respondents also indicated having technical roles prior to DevRel, with 57.9% coming from Engineering (41.6%) or Development (16.3%), the top two categories. Other roles like Technical Trainer, Solution Architect, Technical Writer, and Program Manager were also common.

You'll often be required to build things and interact with developers. While you may not need to have deep domain knowledge in your specific technical niche, your job is to ask the questions others might shy away from and find the answers, so your community doesn't have to. Even with AI tools like GitHub Copilot and <u>Cursor.ai</u> making it easier to build demos, having a technical background means you'll learn faster and won't be starting from zero.

As additional evidence, here is text pulled directly from GitLab's candidacy requirements for their developer advocates(3):

"You are obsessed with making developers happy. You were a full-time developer in a previous life (or you've been through bootcamps and know how to program and code with the best of 'em!), but you prefer to work with the developer community to improve experience and support through education."

2.2.2 Content

Content is the most valuable asset of a developer advocate job. In the same 2024 State of Developer Relations Survey, when DevRel professionals were asked which activities they spend the most time on, Content Development emerged as the top priority, as shown in Table 2-1.

Table 2-1. *Top activities in DevRel, sourced from the 2024 State of Developer Relations Report*

Top Activities	% of Respondents
Content development - Education - videos, workshops, tutorials, webinars, etc.	50.3%
Content development - Technical - Docs, Getting Started Guides, etc.	43.5%
Advocacy - liaison with developers and deliver feedback to internal teams	43.2%
Events - Public speaking	40.3%
Content development - Marketing - blogs, websites, marketing materials	31.6%
Strategy and planning	27.4%
Developer Experience - SDK creation, API governance, Developer tools, etc.	24.5%
Managing online communities	20.3%
Managing program and team	19%
Events - Organizing your own (conferences, workshops, etc.)	17.4%
Content production	17.1%
Research / Staying up to date	14.2%
Internal company relations	12.9%
Events - Attending	12.7%
Social media	12.3%
Data collection and reporting	11.9%
Marketing and outreach	11.9%
Events - Booth Management	10.6%
Support - answering support tickets, forum questions	10.6%
Customer success	10.6%
Product development	9.7%
Managing champion or ambassador programs	7.4%
Events - Sponsoring	6.1%

This is why this book focuses heavily on the development, creation, execution, and distribution of content as a key driver of developer advocacy roles, because content creation is the most significant function of Developer Advocate Individual Contributors.

In developer advocacy, various forms of content are essential for engaging with the developer community. This includes everything from Technical Blog Posts, Documentation, and Video Tutorials, to Webinars, Live Coding Sessions, Case Studies, Sample Code Repositories, Podcasts, Cheat Sheets, Infographics, Newsletters, Social Media Posts, Interactive Workshops, and Online Courses, among others.

I won't spend too much time discussing content here because the rest of the book will cover everything you need to know about content in the context of developer advocacy.

2.2.3 Community

This is an excerpt from an Auth0 Developer Advocate job posting:

> *"Developer advocates have two main focuses. The first is to educate developers about Auth0 by Okta and identity through speaking at events, creating live and recorded video content, writing, appearing on podcasts, and other creative mediums within your community. The second is to serve the larger developer community by answering questions and listening to feedback at events, on forums, GitHub, social media, and Slack and Discord servers. You will then take that information and share it with other marketing, engineering, and documentation teams at Auth0 to help improve our developer experience."*

At its core, developer advocacy is a two-way function. On one side, you create and share content with your community to attract, engage, and drive adoption. On the other, you listen and carry their feedback back into the company, shaping the product, docs, and developer experience.

Ideally, that loop should be balanced: half outbound and half inbound. In reality, many teams tilt heavily toward outbound, spending 95% of their energy on pushing content and only 5% on bringing insights back. The best advocates work to restore the balance, ensuring the developer's voice flows inward as strongly as the company's message flows outward.

The code and content function of developer advocates is centered around engaging, serving, and nurturing a community.

"... Developer Advocates understand our community, their problems, and how GitLab can solve them."

When I talk about "community," I'm not only referring to your active users or customers, or even the support forums, Discord servers, or Slack groups built around your product. Community is also more than your social media followers or newsletter subscribers. These are important, but they make up only your immediate community. Beyond them lies a broader network of developers such as prospective customers, partners, influencers, and others who also shape the ecosystem around your product.

Still, your community does not encompass every developer out there. It specifically consists of the segment of developers for whom your product was designed, the ones who face the problems your product is built to solve.

Attempting to target "all developers" is a waste of time and resources as illustrated in Figure 2-1. The developer pool is vast, comprising millions of individuals with different skill levels, authority, technology stacks, and programming languages. They live in different regions, speak different languages, work in different company contexts, and pursue different goals. No single message will resonate with them all, and not all of them need your product in the first place.

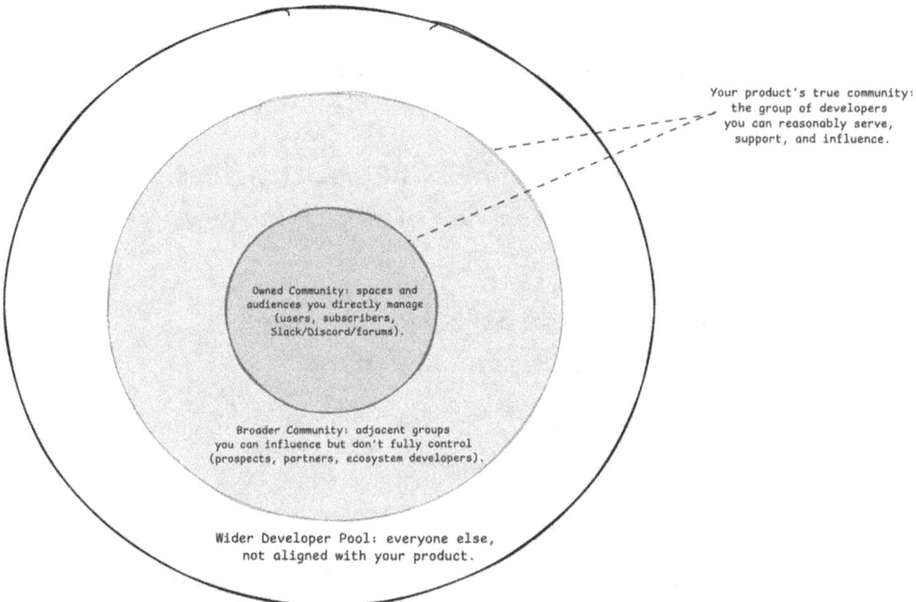

Figure 2-1. *Layers of a Developer Community, illustrating the relationship between your owned community, broader ecosystem, and the wider developer pool*

To be effective as a developer advocate, you must deeply understand your product's true community; their experiences, capabilities, expectations, needs, and problems, and how your product can address those gaps.

While creating content is central to developer advocacy, the most impactful content is born from actively listening to your community. A helpful metaphor is to think of community as the roots of a tree. Just as roots nourish and sustain growth, the community provides the input and feedback that give your advocacy efforts meaning. You need to understand your community on several levels:

- **Their motivation**: Why do they do what they do?

- **Their skillset**: What tools and resources do they currently use, what gaps do they have?

- **Their goals**: What do they want to achieve?

- **Their mindset**: How do they evaluate and make decisions?

- **The demands on their time**: Where and how do they need support? What type of projects are they working on?

- **Their limiting factors**: Skills, budget, existing infrastructure choices, corporate culture?

- **The demands on their attention**: Who are you competing with for mindshare?

- And where to find them?

This book does not cover how to become a developer, because the assumption is that you already have software development skills before picking it up.

However, In Part II, Chapter 3, we'll look at tactics for active listening and how to uncover the problems your community cares about most. Later, in Part III, Chapter 7, we'll talk about how to leverage your communities to scale the impact of your work.

2.3 Reality Check: Developer Advocacy May Not Be Right for You

"Developer advocacy isn't for everyone. If you're uncomfortable in the spotlight, feel drained after public speaking, or struggle with multitasking, this role might not be your thing. It may not be your cup of tea if you prefer deep tech dives over explanations, or find keeping up with tech trends a chore. Developer advocacy is very public-facing and requires constant adaptation. But don't worry if it doesn't feel right - there

are related roles that might suit you better. For instance, a Developer Educator focuses more on content creation with less travel, while a Developer Relations Engineer improves user experience with less public-facing work. The key is to be honest about what you enjoy and what drains you. It's all about finding the right fit for your skills and personality." ~ **Gift Egwenu, Senior Developer Advocate**

If you're looking for a role where you just get assigned tasks, put on your headphones, and code all day, developer advocacy might not be the right fit for you. This isn't a job for those who prefer to play behind the scenes.

I often have friends who are full-time developers tell me their work has become a bit monotonous, and they want to add some excitement to their lives. The next thing I hear is, "What's it like being a developer advocate? It seems pretty exciting, maybe I should switch."

Sure, developer advocacy can be exciting and even glamorous at times, especially when you see advocates traveling the world to speak at conferences. But that's only part of the story. Along with the excitement comes a lot of uncertainty and the need to be comfortable working in grey areas. It wouldn't be fair to gloss over the challenges and intricacies that come with this career path.

2.3.1 It Requires Comfort with Ambiguity

Developer advocacy is full of open-ended tasks. If you don't enjoy open-ended tasks like "go make people aware of our company," or if you struggle in environments where there are no clear best practices or definitive answers, you might want to reconsider this path. If you prefer clear boundaries, defined responsibilities, and knowing exactly what's expected of you so you can complete your tasks and head home, then this may not be the right career for you.

2.3.2 It's a Public-Facing Role

This is not a role you can hide in. You'll be constantly explaining your work and often justifying your impact, especially at companies where DevRel is not well understood. Being comfortable in the public eye is essential. That doesn't mean you must be a natural-born speaker or a prolific writer, but you do need to communicate clearly, listen actively, and make others feel heard. Teaching—whether through talks, blogs, or videos—is a big part of the job. If the thought of being visible drains you, this role may not be a match.

2.3.3 It Involves Constant Multitasking and Context Switching

In developer advocacy, you need to be an efficient multitasker, comfortable managing several projects simultaneously, often requiring completely different skill sets. For example, at any given time, I'm juggling five different work projects. I might be testing a new feature, creating a slide deck for a conference, recording a tutorial video, and putting together a quarterly report on program metrics, or drafting a content strategy for the next month, which all require rapid context switching and diverse skillsets. It can feel like juggling five jobs at once, each with a different skill set.

2.3.4 Career Progression Isn't Always Clear

Developer advocacy is still a relatively young field. Not every company has a clear career ladder for it, which means you may need to advocate for yourself. That requires initiative: asking for feedback, negotiating your growth path, and being comfortable with ambiguity not just in your daily work but in your career as a whole.

2.3.5 You Might Lose Your Technical Edge

Another thing to consider is that, as a full-time developer advocate, you might find yourself falling behind technically over the years. Unlike in engineering, where you'll frequently get to solve complex problems, a lot of your time in developer advocacy might be spent building demos or creating content that sparks that "aha" light bulb and shows your developer community what's possible with a tool. If you want to keep your technical edge, you'll need to be proactive and make an effort to engage with complex problems outside of your regular duties. You might not be coding daily, so you need to constantly upskill.

Summary

Developer advocacy is a role without a fixed blueprint. It spans three specialties: code, content, and community. What you actually do will depend on your strengths and the needs of your company and developers.

But while the job can look glamorous from the outside, the reality is more complex. Success requires comfort with ambiguity, constant context-switching, and the willingness to be a public-facing communicator. In the end, it's not the right fit for everyone.

Despite these challenges, the rewards can be profound. Sometimes it is quick, like helping someone fix an issue in minutes. Sometimes it is big, like standing in a packed room where every seat is filled, with people listening intently to you while you talk. And often it is lasting, like hearing that your tutorial helped someone land their first job or that your work made another developer's life easier. More than anything, the most meaningful reward is connection: seeing how your work sparks momentum for others and contributes to a stronger developer community.

PART II

Advocating to Developers

Most developer advocacy programs today share a common set of goals: drive awareness, increase adoption, reduce churn, and support the broader developer community. But if you zoom out, all of these roll up into one deeper purpose: **enablement.**

Enablement is fundamentally about helping developers succeed. That means guiding them to discover the product, showing them how to use it effectively, and removing the friction that keeps them from getting value.

To do that, three things have to happen:

1. **Awareness**: Developers must know your product exists and can solve their problems. Blog posts, videos, presentations, social media, and podcast appearances all introduce developers to your technology.

2. **Resources**: Once interested, developers need documentation, best practices guides, and onboarding materials to help them integrate and effectively use your product.

3. **Engagement**: While adopting your tool, developers must connect with your community to build expertise and confidence. They need opportunities to ask questions, get support when blocked, and provide feedback that improves the product for everyone.

Content powers each of those steps.

It's not surprising. Content is the most scalable way to achieve product enablement. Unlike 1:1 interactions, a single tutorial, demo, or blog post can help thousands of developers across time zones, long after you've moved on to something else. This is why, according to the 2025 State of Developer Relations Survey, at most companies, content is where developer advocates spend the bulk of their time.

The format and scope may vary, but it is still content. At companies with structured DevRel teams, entry-level developer advocates spend most of their time on content that supports marketing. Mid-level advocates focus more on educational materials like tutorials, workshops, and webinars. Principal level ICs dedicate much of their time to content strategy.

But not all content is created equal. Some content gets ignored. Some attract attention but drive no action. And some content, crafted with the right strategy, becomes the reason developers adopt your tool, tell their team about it, and come back for more.

This section is about building that kind of content. Not by copying formats or chasing trends but by building a developer advocacy strategy that's deeply aligned with your company, your product, and your users.

In this section, we'll explore how to develop an effective developer advocacy strategy, particularly if you're joining a company where individual contributors must take initiative.

Chapter 3 will guide you through laying the groundwork for your developer advocacy strategy, helping you understand the key stakeholders that should influence it: your company, the product, the users, and your team. Chapter 4 will then walk you through translating those insights into a practical strategy, including defining your content focus. Chapter 5 will cover best practices and tooling for producing engaging technical content, including how to navigate AI in your content workflow. Finally, Chapter 6 will cover how to measure the impact and success of your advocacy efforts through metrics.

Let's dive in.

CHAPTER 3

Laying the Groundwork for Your Developer Advocacy Strategy

One of the most common struggles for new developer advocates is figuring out where to start. You join a company, you're handed a product, and the unspoken expectation is: go do DevRel. So you start writing blog posts, maybe spin up a Discord, and apply to speak at a few conferences. But in the back of your mind, a question keeps surfacing: *Am I even doing the right thing?*

That question usually creeps in when there's no clear strategy, no shared sense of purpose, and no map connecting your day-to-day efforts with what the company actually needs.

This chapter is about building that map.

Your job in developer advocacy is not just to write helpful tutorials or represent the company at events. Your job is to help developers succeed with your product in a way that also helps your company succeed. That means you need a strategy rooted in reality. Your work needs to align with the business, the product, the users, and your team to drive any valuable impact.

© Linda Ikechukwu 2026

L. Ikechukwu, *A Friendly Guide to Developer Advocacy*, Friendly Guides to Technology,
https://doi.org/10.1007/979-8-8688-2462-3_3

By the end of this chapter, you'll have a clearer sense of what actually matters. You'll stop guessing. You'll stop throwing content at the wall. And you'll start crafting a strategy that helps developers, the company, and you as a developer advocate grow.

3.1 First, Understand the Company

Before you set out to build a developer advocacy strategy, you need to understand one thing above all else: what kind of company you're building it for. What does the company actually care about? How does it make money? And what kind of change does it want to drive in the world?

A good developer advocacy strategy doesn't live in a vacuum. It lives in the messy middle of a company's priorities, business model, growth stage, and internal politics. If you skip this step and jump straight into content creation, you might build things that look useful but don't move the needle. You might focus on metrics that sound impressive but don't map to any real goal. That's how DevRel becomes a feel-good department instead of a high-impact one.

Grounding your strategy in business context does more than just protect the integrity of your role.

- You gain clarity and direction.

- You waste less time on low-impact work.

- You can demonstrate how your work supports real outcomes.

- You collaborate better across the company.

And where do you start? You start by analyzing your company's **role in the market**, its **business model and monetization strategy**, its **growth stage and funnel focus**, and finally, its **orientation toward developers**, whether it's a developer-first company or a developer-plus one.

Each of these layers gives you context that sharpens your strategy. The best DevRel work doesn't just reflect what developers want; it also reflects what the company needs. Your job is to find the overlap.

3.1.1 What Is the Company's Position in the Market?

Before you decide what kind of developer advocacy efforts to focus on, you need to understand the game your company is playing. Not every company is trying to do the same thing in the market at the same time. Some are defending an established position. Others are trying to break into the market and challenge incumbents. Some are focused on serving a narrow niche. Others are racing to gain traction before time or funding runs out. These differences shape what matters, what success looks like, and how quickly you are expected to deliver results. As shown in Table 3-1, each of these scenarios comes with different risks, opportunities, and expectations that should shape how your developer advocacy operates.

Market Leaders

These companies already dominate their space. They're not trying to prove themselves. They're trying to scale sustainably, deepen trust, and maintain leadership. That means developer advocacy here often focuses on polish:refining documentation, improving onboarding, supporting large-scale events, and building robust community infrastructure. You're working to keep developers engaged and successful at scale.

As a developer advocate in a market-leading company, your work will likely be more mature, more structured, and more visible. There's also more pressure to align with the brand and uphold the trust the company has earned.

Challengers

These companies are ambitious. These companies are going head-to-head with the market leaders, often differentiating through pricing, modern UX, or a focused feature set. They must demonstrate to developers their superiority.

Developer advocacy at a challenger company is often about contrast, i.e highlighting what you do differently, better, or faster. You'll spend time identifying pain points in dominant tools, positioning your product as the modern alternative, and enabling developers to make the switch.

In this position, your content needs to speak directly to disillusionment. "We know what you hate about the old way; here's how we fix it."

Niche Players

Some companies would rather not serve everyone. They go deep instead of wide, solving highly specific problems for a tightly defined group. They serve a focused audience or solve a specific slice of the puzzle.

If your company is a niche player, your strategy should be focused and sharp. You don't need to be everywhere. You just need to be indispensable to your slice of the market.

Developer advocacy in a niche company is about expertise and community. You're speaking the language of your audience with precision. You're building content that feels like it could only have been written by someone inside the space.

Shooting Stars

These are the early-stage or fast-growing startups that are still figuring things out. They're new or fast-growing players gaining traction by offering a fresh take or targeting an underserved segment.

Maybe the product is new, the team is small, and the messaging is changing every few weeks. It's chaotic. Developer advocacy here is about velocity. They need visibility, rapid feedback loops, and developer goodwill. You'll likely spend time seeding communities, generating awareness, and smoothing over onboarding.

You will assume various roles such as writer, speaker, support representative, community manager, and product tester, and your contributions will significantly influence the direction of the company. If you thrive in ambiguity and love helping shape a company's narrative from the ground up, this is where developer advocacy gets thrilling.

As of the time of writing this book, I currently work as a Lead Developer Advocate for a company that would be classified as a shooting star, Smallstep Labs.

Table 3-1. *Market Positioning in the Observability Ecosystem, comparing four companies by their market position, key characteristics, target audience, and DevRel focus. The table highlights how each company's Developer Relations strategy aligns with its position in the competitive landscape*

Market Positioning in the Observability Ecosystem

Company	Market Role	Key Characteristics	Target Audience	DevRel Focus
New Relic	Market Leader	Long established in application performance monitoring; widely adopted across enterprises	Enterprise IT teams	Refining experience; improving developer onboarding; building stronger community programs
Chronosphere	Challenger	High-scale observability platform built on open-source M3; positions as cost-efficient, high-performance alternative	Enterprises looking for alternatives to established vendors	Differentiation content; demonstrating advantages in performance and cost efficiency
Sentry	Niche Player	Specializes in error tracking and performance monitoring; tight focus on specific developer needs	Frontend and mobile developers	Depth over breadth; expert guidance and domain-specific tooling
SigNoz	Shooting Star	Open-source observability platform; self-hosted alternative to commercial tools; native OpenTelemetry support	Developers seeking open-source, self-hosted solutions	Generating awareness; seeding communities; smoothing onboarding; collecting rapid feedback

3.1.2 What Is the Company's Growth Stage?

If understanding your company's market position helps you see how loudly you need to speak, understanding its growth stage tells you where to point the megaphone.

Different stages of company growth come with different goals and different expectations for developer advocacy. A seed-stage startup hunting for product-market fit won't need the same kind of support as a Series D company trying to reduce churn and expand its enterprise footprint.

Likewise, some companies need help attracting new developers at the top of the funnel, while others are focused on retaining and activating the ones they already have.

Your strategy only works if it meets the company where it is.

The AAARRRP growth funnel framework (Figure 3-1), introduced by Phil Leggetter (`https://www.leggetter.co.uk/`) and adapted from Dave McClure's AARRR "Pirate Metrics" model (2007), breaks down the customer life cycle into stages—Awareness, Acquisition, Activation, Retention, Revenue, Referral, and Product feedback—that help companies answer a crucial question: Which stage matters most for our growth right now?

The AAARRRP Framework
(Growth Funnel)

Figure 3-1. *The AAARRRP Framework showing how company focus shifts across growth stages*

Early-stage companies usually focus at the top of the funnel, building awareness and driving acquisition. Growth-phase companies lean into the middle, emphasizing activation and retention. Mature companies often concentrate at the bottom, where revenue expansion, referrals, and product feedback loops sustain long-term growth.

Mapping your developer advocacy strategy to both your company's growth stage and the funnel brings clarity. It shows whether you should spend most of your limited time on top-of-funnel awareness content, mid-funnel onboarding, or bottom-funnel enablement.

Early-Stage Startups

At this stage, the company is usually trying to figure out who it's for and whether the product even solves a real problem. Developer advocates here are part educator, part researcher, and part community builder. You will likely be a one-person team, and you'll not just be broadcasting; you'd also be listening closely, taking in feedback, and helping the product team close the gap between intention and reality.

At this stage the company might be trying to get more people in the door, which hinges on top-of-funnel work. You should prioritize

- Generating awareness among early adopters

- Surfacing real-world feedback to influence product development

- Creating lightweight educational content to test messaging and positioning

- Building personal relationships with users who might become early champions

Growth-Phase Companies

These companies have some traction and are now trying to scale it. The product works. The team knows who they're building for. The challenge now is reaching more people, enabling more teams, and making the developer journey repeatable and smooth. They will be trying to turn interest into sustained use, and that falls under mid-funnel, that is, onboarding, integration guides, and activation support.

As a developer advocate here, you should probably prioritize

- Standardizing onboarding and educational flows

- Producing scalable content for common use cases

- Identifying the sticking points in the adoption journey

- Reducing friction that causes churn

- Supporting community-driven efforts that reinforce growth

Mature Companies

At this point, growth tends to slow down. The company is likely invested in looking for new markets, reducing churn, or improving operational efficiency. Developer advocates in mature companies often shift from generating top-of-funnel awareness to supporting mid- and bottom-of-funnel needs.

As a developer advocate here, you should probably prioritize things like:

- Enabling long-term users with more advanced content

- Creating case studies or integration guides for enterprise adoption

- Supporting internal teams (sales, success, support) with technical validation

- Community engagement

Table 3-2 inspired by Naomi Pentrel maps some common Developer Advocacy initiatives to stages of the AAARRP funnel framework. It should help you see or decide what activities to prioritize or focus on.

Table 3-2. *Common Developer Advocacy initiatives mapped to stages of the AAARRRP framework*

	Awareness	Acquisition	Activation	Retention	Revenue	Referral	Product
Docs & Reference Guides / How tos		x	x				
Library development			x				x
Quick start apps			x				x
Blog posts, Tutorials, Hacks	x	x	x	x			
Webinars	x	x	x	x			
Event/Meetup Sponsorship	x	x					
Talks, Meetups, Conferences	x	x					
Support, Zendesk, StackOverflow, Forums			x	x			x
Pre-sales technical discussion		x	x				
Alpha/Beta Programs			x				
Office Hours			x	x			
Capture developer feedback							x
Help company recruitment		x					
Ambassador programs						x	

Notice how there are no points for Revenue in Table 3-2? That's because, in my opinion, developer advocacy should not drive nor be measured by revenue; that's the job of sales. What developer advocacy should be measured by is sales or revenue-enablement.

And of course, the AAARRP framework maps to the developer journey stages of Discover, Evaluate, Learn, Build, and Scale, which we discussed in Chapter 1 (as shown in Table 3-3). The most effective developer advocacy work happens when you choose activities that match your company's growth goals and also target the exact stage where developers are struggling with your product. When these two things align, you meet developers where they are and help them succeed, while also driving business goals at the same time.

Table 3-3. *Mapping the Developer Journey to the AAARRRP framework, showing how each stage aligns with developer behaviors and business growth outcomes*

Developer Journey	AAARRRP Stage	Explanation
Discover	Awareness	Do developers know we exist? Example: A developer first learns your product exists (blog, conference talk, tweet, SEO, word of mouth).
Evaluate	Acquisition	Are they signing up or trying the product? Example: They try it out for the first time, maybe sign up or look at docs, deciding if it's worth more time.
Learn	Activation	Are they reaching the "aha" moment quickly? Example: They hit their first "aha" moment; a successful API call, Hello World app, or working tutorial.
Build	Retention	Do they keep coming back and deepening usage? They keep coming back to build real projects, moving past demos into actual use.
Scale	Revenue + Product	Does their usage translate into paying accounts or product expansion from feedback? Example: Their use grows in size or complexity. This may trigger revenue (enterprise adoption, paid plans) and product feedback (features needed for scaling).
Refer	Referral	Are they telling others about us? They become advocates, telling colleagues, writing blog posts, or speaking about the product at meetups.

Note   Position in the market refers to your company's external positioning. That is, how it is perceived relative to others in the ecosystem. Growth stage, on the other hand, describes internal maturity: where the company is in its life cycle financially, structurally, and strategically.

A market leader might still be early-stage in a new region. A niche player might be a long-established business. A shooting star might still be pre-revenue. The distinction matters: external position shapes your messaging, while internal maturity shapes your priorities.

It's also worth noting that position in the market can apply not just to a company, but to a specific product. A company might be a market leader overall while launching a new product that enters the market as a challenger.

For example, AmazonAmazon is a dominant cloud provider with AWS, but when it launched Honeycode, its no-code app builder, it was entering a crowded space already served by established tools like Airtable and Notion. So while Amazon was a market leader, Honeycode was a challenger product.

As you analyze your company's product in the next section, take time to consider how that product is positioned within its space, even if the company itself has a different position.

3.1.3 What Is the Company's Business Model/ Monetization Strategy

If their position in the market tells you how your company shows up in the world, the monetization strategy tells you how it makes money, and the business model tells you who gives it that money.

There are two fundamental business models in the developer tools space: Developer-First and Developer-Plus. In a Developer-First company, developers are the primary customer. The product is built for them, sold to them, and succeeds or fails based on their experience. In a Developer-Plus company, developers are not the end customer. Instead, they enable or extend the business's reach to a broader market. Table 3-4 breaks down the key differences between the two. The business model directly shapes the monetization strategy. Developer-First companies monetize through direct developer adoption, either up front or delayed, while Developer-Plus companies monetize through the broader value that developer enablement creates. Each model changes how you measure success and helps you understand what kind of impact stakeholders expect, even if they don't say it directly. Here is a look at the most common monetization strategies used by companies that fall under the two different business models and what each one means for your developer advocacy work.

Revenue Up Front

For some developer-first companies, revenue is tied directly to product usage. Think of SaaS subscriptions, pay-as-you-go pricing, or seat-based licenses. The customer commits early, often after a short trial. In these companies, developer advocacy is usually expected to **accelerate time-to-value**. The faster a developer goes from "trying" to "using," the better.

Here, you'd find success and make more impact in activities like removing friction in onboarding, creating momentum through quickstarts and integrations, and reducing dropout by offering clear, confident support through documentation or a community forum.

Revenue Delayed

Some developer-first companies have products with long adoption arcs. Think Open-source tools with enterprise offerings, or freemium products that monetize later through support plans or hosted services, or API companies that charge based on usage once developers reach production scale fall under this category.

Stripe, for example, might not see revenue from a developer until that developer builds something successful and monetizes it.

In these cases, developer advocacy needs to focus on community building, long-term trust, and broad education. You're planting seeds that may take months or years to grow. That means success depends more on adoption and stickiness than on short-term revenue.

Market Enhancement

Market enhacement is one of the revenue strategies used by developer-plus companies. Since they cannot monetize through developer adoption directly, the business invests in developer tools and resources because doing so expands the market for their core product. developers aren't always the end customer. Instead, developers enable or extend the business's reach. Think of banks offering APIs, hardware companies offering SDKs, or telcos building developer portals.

For example, NVIDIA's core business revolves around selling hardware like GPUs, but it invests heavily in tools, SDKs, and libraries for developers, such as CUDA, TensorRT, and Omniverse. They do this not because those tools directly generate revenue, but because they expand the ecosystem and encourage developers to build in ways that ultimately drive demand for NVIDIA hardware. Their developer efforts are designed to **enhance the market** for their core product line by enabling innovation and making their platform indispensable across industries like AI, robotics, gaming, and scientific computing

In this revenue model, developer advocacy is often part of a broader influence strategy. You'd find success in making the product approachable, showing off integrations, and making developers feel confident embedding it into their stack.

Ecosystem Play

Ecosystem Play is a monetization strategy used by Developer-Plus companies that rely on developers to build the next layer of value. Think platforms like Salesforce, Shopify, or Unity, which depend on an ecosystem of third-party apps and plugins to stay relevant. Their growth comes from empowering developers to extend what's possible on their platforms.

Developer advocacy here would find success in enablement, trust, and showcasing success. You'll create example apps, run community programs, and support builders as they go to market. You might not be optimizing for revenue directly, but you're building the surface area where future revenue is created.

Table 3-4. *Comparison between Developer-First and Developer-Plus companies*

Characteristic	Developer-First Company	Developer-Plus Company
Core audience	Developers	Developers + business stakeholders
Revenue model	Directly tied to developer adoption	Broader B2B/B2C monetization
Product interface	Code-first, built for devs	May include SDKs, APIs, or dev portals
DevRel focus	Community, adoption, feedback, scale	Enablement, Integrations, cross-functional impact
Internal positioning	Core to product growth	One function among many

3.2 Second, Understand the Product

Before you can explain a product to anyone else, you need to know it yourself. Not vaguely. Not from a Notion doc or sales one-pager. You need to know it in your bones from using it, breaking it, and shipping something real with it.

This is the first responsibility of developer advocacy. Your credibility begins here. If you don't understand how the product works, what it enables, where it shines, and where it breaks, you can't advocate for it with any real authority. You're just repeating slogans. That might pass in marketing, but it won't fly with developers.

Understanding the product means asking the kinds of questions developers ask: What can I build with this? What problems does it actually solve? Where does it sit in my stack? What are the trade-offs? It means exploring not just the functionality but also the expectations that come with its category. An SDK is expected to work out of the box. A framework is expected to provide structure. A service is expected to scale. If your product doesn't meet those expectations, or if it does something better, you need to know that, and you need to be able to explain why.

Because until you understand the product, honestly and thoroughly, like a developer would, you can't create content that helps people use it. You can't advocate for it with trust. And you definitely can't shape a strategy that drives adoption. So start here. Get to know the thing you're championing.

3.2.1 Learn the Product Category

The first step is to step back and understand what kind of product you're advocating for.

Is your product an API, an SDK, a CLI tool, a framework, or a hosted service? Does it integrate directly into an app or wrap around it? Is it something developers run locally, or a platform they push code to? These distinctions matter because of what they say about the *developer experience* your users will expect.

When you know what category your product falls under, you are also able to map where your product fits in a typical dev stack. Does it run at build time, deploy time, or runtime? Is it part of the development environment, or something that lives in staging and production? Does it touch infrastructure, authentication, testing, analytics, or something else entirely?

Knowing this helps you map

- **Dependencies**: What needs to be in place before someone can use it? What infrastructure or knowledge will one need before they can even begin?

- **Integration points**: What tools or frameworks can your product integrate or interoperate with? Because developers aren't just asking what your product does. They're asking where it fits in their work.

- **Developer mindset**: When will they think about your product? When they're scaffolding a new project? When they're debugging an issue? When they're scaling?

All this helps you decide what kind of content to create, what kind of integrations to prioritize, and what kind of mental model to reinforce in the way you teach and explain the product.

Here are some common developer product categories and what they typically imply. Note that many products span multiple categories. A company might offer APIs, SDKs, and a CLI tool all as part of the same platform, but understanding each category helps you recognize what kind of DevRel work each component requires.

APIs

Examples: Stripe, Twilio, Plaid

DevRel focus: Docs, SDKs, sample apps, Postman collections, quickstarts, reference guides, debugging support

APIs are the bread and butter of developer tools. They're meant to be integrated into other codebases, which means developers care most about clarity, reliability, and usability.

As a developer advocate working on an API, your job isn't just to make sure the docs are correct. You need to make them useful. This means focusing on use-case-driven examples, showing how different endpoints work together, and providing real-world guides that answer the question, "How do I do X with this API?"

Developer advocacy in this space means

- Creating clear, accurate reference documentation with real-world examples

- Building sample applications that showcase multiple API endpoints working together

- Developing SDK wrappers in popular languages to improve developer experience

- Maintaining Postman collections, Swagger docs, or other interactive exploration tools

- Monitoring and improving error messages and debugging flows

You also have to think in ecosystems. Is there an official SDK for the API? Are there community-built wrappers available for other languages? Are there tutorials in languages beyond just JavaScript or Python? These are all things DevRel can help shape.

SDKs

Examples: Firebase SDKs, Mapbox SDKs, Auth0 SDKs

DevRel focus: Tutorials by language, platform-specific guides, starter templates, SDK changelogs, community SDK contributions

SDKs (Software Development Kits) are like ready-to-use power tools. They're designed to make developers productive quickly by abstracting complexity and offering language-specific building blocks. Unlike raw APIs that require manual wiring, SDKs provide a smoother, often more opinionated developer experience.

When you're advocating for an SDK, your job is to reduce the distance between "I want to build this" and "It's working." That means focusing on clarity, coverage, and context. Is the SDK well-documented across the most-used languages? Are there good examples that show how to integrate it into common frameworks and stacks? Is there a sandbox or playground environment to experiment in?

Your DevRel work here might involve

- Maintaining starter kits in multiple languages

- Writing guides for common integrations ("Using the SDK with Next.js")

- Recording walkthrough videos that show real implementation steps

- Collecting developer feedback on edge cases and confusing APIs

The easier you make it to get from zero to "it works," the more successful the SDK and your advocacy will be.

Developer Tools

Examples: ESLint, GitHub CLI, Docker

DevRel focus: Onboarding flows, productivity tips, configuration guides, integration with editors/IDEs, plugin tutorials

Developer tools are often local-first, integrated into a developer's everyday workflow. These could be command-line tools, language plugins, linters, debuggers, testing utilities, or code generators. Unlike APIs and SDKs, they're usually not about enabling a new capability. They're about improving efficiency, confidence, and flow. They're software that help developers write, debug, or deploy code more efficiently.

The bar here is high. Developers will adopt tools that feel snappy, don't fight their mental model, and integrate smoothly into the way they already work. If you mess up the onboarding experience or force them to rewire their workflow, they'll abandon it fast.

Developer advocacy in this space means

- Providing minimal-setup guides or install scripts

- Creating "how I use this" blog posts or short screencasts from real-world use

- Gathering feedback from early adopters and piping it back to engineering

- Highlighting edge cases, portability concerns, or integrations with editors and CI tools

You're also often involved in improving docs, shaping developer experience, and providing context to engineering teams on user behavior.

Developer Services

Examples: Supabase, Vercel, Cloudflare Workers

DevRel focus: Time-to-value demos, templates, integrations, real-world apps, performance and scalability education

Developer services are hosted platforms or products that provide infrastructure, tooling, or other capabilities through an interface (usually a dashboard, CLI, or API). Think Supabase, Auth0, Stripe, or Render. These services abstract away complexity and let developers focus on business logic.

The promise of a developer service is: You don't have to build this yourself. We've already done it. The trade-off is trust: the developer is outsourcing critical parts of their stack. They need to know that the service is reliable, secure, well-supported, and able to scale with their needs.

Developer advocates here help build that trust through

- Demos and quickstarts that show off the speed to value

- Case studies and success stories that show who's using it and how

- Sample apps that show how to build real things end-to-end

- Educational content that explains the trade-offs and edge cases clearly

Your job is to shorten the "time to first wow," remove friction, and show developers how to build with the service safely and effectively.

Developer Marketplaces and Ecosystems

Examples: GitHub Marketplace, Figma Plugins, Salesforce AppExchange

DevRel focus: Contributor onboarding, programmatic standards, API integration support, discoverability, and trust-building in the ecosystem

Marketplaces and platforms like GitHub, npm, Figma plugins, or even game engines like Unity create ecosystems. These aren't just tools. They're networks. Your community includes developers who build on the platform and those who consume those creations.

The advocacy work here is multi-layered. You might be

- Educating creators on how to build and publish high-quality packages or extensions

- Helping consumers discover useful tools through curated content or recommendation systems

- Supporting contribution programs or open-source maintainers

- Running contests, ambassador programs, or spotlight campaigns

In a marketplace, developer advocacy isn't just about helping one kind of user. It's about creating a healthy feedback loop between creators and consumers, and making the whole ecosystem more vibrant.

3.2.2 Learn the Product Like a Developer

The next step is to understand the product and to use it like a developer would. Not like someone preparing a demo but like someone with a real problem to solve and a finite amount of patience.

Get your hands dirty. Install it. Use it. Build something real, even if it's small. Try to accomplish a typical task a new user would attempt. Then keep going until something breaks or becomes frustrating. That's where the learning starts.

If you're already familiar with the product, try to use it like a beginner. If you're new to it, even better. You have the advantage of a beginner's mind. Walk through the onboarding flow. Try to integrate it into a sample app. Watch where things break. Try the quickstart guide on a clean machine. Pay attention to where your instincts as a developer align with the product's flow and where they don't.

And don't stop with your experience. Watch how new users interact with the product. Observe their questions in your community forums or Discord. Read GitHub issues. Search for patterns.

This kind of profound product understanding isn't just a personal exercise; it's the foundation of every content decision you make, every event talk you give, and every conversation you have with a new user. Once you truly know what the product does and how it fits into a developer's workflow, you can begin to speak with clarity, not just about how it works but also about why it matters.

As you do this, keep a record of what you notice. Focus on three categories (adapted from Sam Julien's "How to Start Doing Dev Rel Right Now" article):

1. **The Wins**: What makes this product delightful? What's fast, clean, or surprisingly helpful? These are the things you'll want to highlight in demos and tutorials because they're often what developers remember, and tell their friends about.

2. **The Friction**: Where do developers hesitate? What makes the setup longer than it should be? What assumptions does the product make that don't hold up in the wild?

3. **The Pain**: What actively hurts the developer experience? These are the blockers, the confusing errors, and the moments that cause people to bounce. If you can find these, document them, and route them to product and engineering teams, you become the bridge between dev frustration and product improvement.

Questions to Ask While Testing

Use this set of questions to guide your discovery:

- Who is this product for? What roles, languages, or frameworks do they use?

- What's the very first thing they'll try to do with it?

- How long does it take to get to a "Wow, this is useful" moment?

- Where do people get stuck? What's confusing or missing?

- What are users trying to build, and how does this product help (or hinder) that?

- What assumptions are baked into the setup, API, or docs?

- What's missing that would make this easier or more powerful?

- Does the product integrate well into common toolchains?

- Does it play nicely with existing workflows or require big changes?

3.2.3 Learn the Competitive Landscape of the Product

Once you've learned how the product works and where it fits in a developer's workflow, you need to zoom out. Products don't exist in a vacuum. Developers always have alternatives, comparisons, and prior experiences that shape how they perceive what you're offering. If your developer advocacy is going to resonate, you need to understand what landscape your product is entering into, and how developers are navigating it.

Understanding the competitive landscape starts with a clear view of the problem your product is trying to solve and then looking at the ecosystem.

- Who else is solving that problem?

- What do their tools look like?

- What expectations do they set?

- And how does your product compare, not just in terms of features but also in developer experience, documentation, setup, flexibility, and philosophy?

The process isn't just about knowing the names of your competitors. It's about understanding how your product is likely to be perceived by someone who has already tried something else. When a developer stumbles across your project, they're not starting from scratch. They're bringing assumptions from the last tool they used, frustrations from the last workflow that broke, and skepticism from the last tool that overpromised.

Look for the Gaps

Go beyond reading feature pages. Use the tools your product competes with. Install them. Read their documentation. Try to build something small.

Sometimes the most strategic thing you can do is focus not on what your competitors do, but on what they don't. Ask

- What workflows are underserved?

- What developer segments feel left out or ignored?

- Where are people hacking things together because the tool wasn't built for their use case?

These gaps are often where small DevRel teams can win. You can create content, tooling, and demos that speak directly to the underserved corners of the market and use them to build trust and traction.

Example: Say you're working on a modern access control product that's competing with long-standing RBAC-focused platforms. Those platforms may dominate the enterprise, but are frustrating for developers building internal tools in fast-moving startups. They might require weeks of YAML wrangling or come with top-heavy policy engines. You might spot a gap like:

> *"No one's really serving frontend-heavy teams who need to ship internal dashboards quickly, but still want robust access control."*

That gap becomes your developer advocacy wedge.

Now you can build out a series:

- A blog post showing access controls from scratch in a fullstack app

- A community guide to securing low-code tools with your product

- A YouTube walkthrough titled "Access Control for the Rest of Us"

Your competitor is still stronger in many areas. That's fine. You're carving a beachhead by spotlighting that your product solves an ignored problem extremely well.

Compare the Developer Experience

Sometimes, the difference is not in what a product does but in how it feels to use. A tool with similar functionality might require a multi-week integration, while yours runs with one install command. That is not a feature, it's a competitive advantage.

Ask

- How easy is it to get started with their tool?

- How fast can you get to a meaningful result?

- How good is their documentation? Support? Community?

Many products win by removing friction, not adding features. If your competitor requires a complex onboarding, and your tool is simple to try in five minutes, you should

- Center your docs around that quick win

- Make a demo that shows the "Wow" moment in 60 seconds

- Write comparison guides that gently highlight what users avoid with your approach

Example: "With Product X, you'll need to write three config files and deploy two services before you get any metrics. With ours, just run npx quick-observe and start tracing instantly."

This is not an attempt to trash the competition. You're showcasing the payoff for switching and giving developers a path to experience it. You're not saying "X is bad." You're saying, "If you've hit these walls with X, here's a different approach."

Be Honest About Strengths and Weaknesses

Your product cannot be the right choice for everyone in all scenarios and use cases. Sometimes, competing products will be better suited, and that's ok.

Turn the lens on your own product. What does it do better than anything else? What kinds of developers or teams are most likely to find success with it? And just as importantly, where does it fall short?

If you ignore the weak spots, you risk overpromising and frustrating new users. If you name them, you build trust. Developers don't expect perfection. They expect honesty and guidance. When you can say, "this works really well in these cases, but you'll want to watch out for X," your content becomes both helpful and credible. The goal is to show where your product provides real leverage, and how developers can take advantage of that.

Feed What Insights Back into the Company

As a developer advocate, you are often one of the few people regularly using competing products and talking directly to developers about their decision-making process. Now that you've done all this research work, bring those insights to your product team about what developers are trying to achieve.

- Share pain points you keep seeing in the community.

- Flag competitor features that developers praise
  (or hate).

- Note where users hit friction that your product could
  easily avoid.

- Help marketing refine positioning with real
  developer quotes.

3.3 Third, Understand Who the Product Is For

"Developers" is not a target audience. It's a demographic category that includes everyone from hobbyists to staff engineers, from solo open-source contributors to enterprise platform teams. A front-end developer at a creative agency is not going to care about your infrastructure policy engine. A staff SRE at a regulated fintech probably won't touch your front-end CMS plugin. If you try to speak to everyone, you will end up resonating with no one.

To be effective in developer advocacy, you need to be precise. You need to understand not just the individuals using your product, but also the organizations they work in, the industries they belong to, and the context in which your product is useful. You're not selling software to personas in a vacuum. You're navigating real company dynamics, industry constraints, and developer motivations that all shape whether your product gets adopted or ignored.

Your marketing team, especially if they have a developer marketing focus, should already have these areas defined as it's imperative for successful marketing. However, if your marketing team does not have defined segmentations, personas, and positioning, you may have to dive in and take the lead.

3.3.1 Start with Segmentation

Segmentation is the process of identifying the types of developers who are most likely to find success with your product. It's not just about job titles or industries. It's about aligning technical requirements, developer goals, organizational constraints, and broader market forces.

You can't build for "all developers." You likely don't have the resources to market to them all, support them all, or serve their needs equally well. That's not a failing. That's focus. Segmentation helps you figure out which developers you can serve well, and which ones you can afford to ignore.

A segmentation framework gives you structure for this kind of thinking. One that works particularly well in developer advocacy is the **Developer Segmentation Framework** (introduced by Caroline Lewko and James Parton in their book, *Developer Relations: How to Build and Grow a Successful Developer Program*) which breaks down your audience into four layers: Technical, User, Organization, and Market.

Technical Layer: What Technical Context Does the Product Require?

What technical conditions need to be in place for someone to use your product?

What languages, frameworks, platforms, or devices are required? What kind of architecture does your tool expect? Does it assume a certain scale, a particular OS, or a specific kind of infrastructure?

If your tool only runs on Linux or integrates with GitHub Actions, that immediately rules out part of the market—and that's a good thing. Every technical constraint helps you narrow the field. You're not trying to serve everyone. You're trying to serve the right people well.

User Layer: Who Is the Developer?

What kind of developers are most likely to succeed with your product?

Are they working solo or in a team? Are they junior or senior? Are they building side projects, running CI pipelines, or making architectural decisions?

Understanding who the user is helps you design better docs, clearer onboarding, and more relevant content. It also helps you avoid mismatches like targeting someone who has no say in whether the tool gets adopted.

Organization Layer: What Kind of Company Are They In?

The developer using your product exists inside an organization. That context matters.

Does your product make more sense in a 10-person startup or a 10,000-person enterprise? Is it meant for teams with formal security policies, or for people prototyping and iterating fast? Is it priced and supported in a way that matches those environments?

This layer also includes the company's structure. Who owns the decision to adopt a new tool? Who approves it? Who uses it day to day? These factors shape everything from your content strategy to your onboarding experience.

Market Layer: What Industry or Region Are They In?

Zooming out even further, some developer segments are shaped by broader market forces.

Regulatory requirements, data sovereignty, legacy infrastructure, and industry-specific workflows all affect adoption. Developers in banking don't operate like developers in gaming. Developers in North America don't always use the same tools or workflows as those in Europe or Asia.

Understanding these market filters helps you target content, select events, and frame messaging with much more precision.

Imagine you're working with a tool that automatically signs Git commits using a hardware-backed certificate. To understand who this product is truly for, you can apply the Developer Segmentation Framework, starting with four key dimensions: technical, user, organizational, and market. Table 3-5 shows what this looks like in practice, applying the four audience layers of the Developer Segmentation Framework to a hardware-backed Git commit signing tool.

Table 3-5. *Example of applying the Developer Segmentation Framework to a hardware-backed Git signing tool*

Layer	Criteria
Technical	CLI-based tool that integrates with GitHub. Requires macOS with Secure Enclave or Windows with TPM. Works best with modern CI systems and assumes developer familiarity with Git internals.
User	Mid-to-senior level engineers, likely in DevOps, security, or infrastructure roles. Comfortable with the terminal, already invested in CI/CD best practices.
Organization	Companies with a maturing or mature security posture. Typically 100+ employees. Likely to have an IT or security team in place, and device management (like MDM) already deployed.
Market	High-trust industries like finance, healthcare, and enterprise tech. Regions with stronger regulatory environments such as North America and Europe.

From a **technical** perspective, this product is CLI-based, integrates best with GitHub, and depends on platform-specific security features like the macOS Secure Enclave or the TPM on Windows. That immediately narrows its fit to developers who are comfortable with the command line and working on supported platforms.

Next is the **user** layer. This tool is likely to be adopted by mid-to-senior level engineers, especially those in roles where security and infrastructure are a priority. Think DevOps, platform engineers, or software engineers who frequently interact with CI/CD systems and care about the integrity of their software supply chain.

At the **organizational** level, your ideal customers are companies with an established or maturing security posture. These are typically companies with at least 100 employees, likely to have an internal IT or security team, and have already rolled out device management systems like MDM or endpoint controls.

And finally, from a **market** standpoint, the strongest fit is with verticals where auditability, regulatory compliance, and security are top of mind. These are industries like financial services, healthcare, and high-trust technology companies. Geographically, this tends to skew toward regions with stricter regulatory frameworks and mature infrastructure, especially North America and parts of Europe.

Once you've built out your developer segments, you're now holding the raw material you need to define your Ideal Customer Profile.

3.3.2 Define Your Ideal Customer Profile (ICP)

Your ICP is not a person. It's not even a developer. It's the type of company where your product fits naturally, delivers clear value, and has the highest likelihood of successful adoption and long-term retention.

Think of your ICP as a composite sketch of the kind of environment where all the right signals line up. The right technical conditions. The right developer roles. The right organizational support. The right market drivers. It's where everything you've learned about your product and your audience comes together.

Let's revisit the Git commit signing tool from the previous example. Based on our segmentation work, we know this product works best in organizations that

- Use GitHub as a primary repo host

- Rely on macOS and Windows machines with built-in secure hardware

- Employ mid-to-senior DevOps or infra engineers

- Have implemented device management tools

- Operate in regulated environments like finance or healthcare

Expanding from that, here's what an ICP might look like:

> A 100+ person financial services company based in North America, using GitHub as its source control platform, managing developer laptops with MDM, and operating under strict compliance requirements. Their engineering team includes dedicated platform and DevSecOps roles, and they are actively investing in supply chain security.

This kind of clarity becomes a north star. It doesn't mean you ignore everyone else. But it gives you something to optimize for. It's the kind of company you build integrations for. The kind of team you write examples for. The kind of use case you prioritize in content, talks, and demos.

It also gives you focus when others in your company start pushing for new audiences. If a team wants to pivot toward SMBs or international developers, you now have a reference point. Does that segment match the profile? If not, what needs to change to make them successful? This doesn't limit your reach, it helps you expand it more intentionally.

The Empathy map canvas (Figure 3-2) by David Gray is an exercise that the company can do, to help with realizing their ICP.

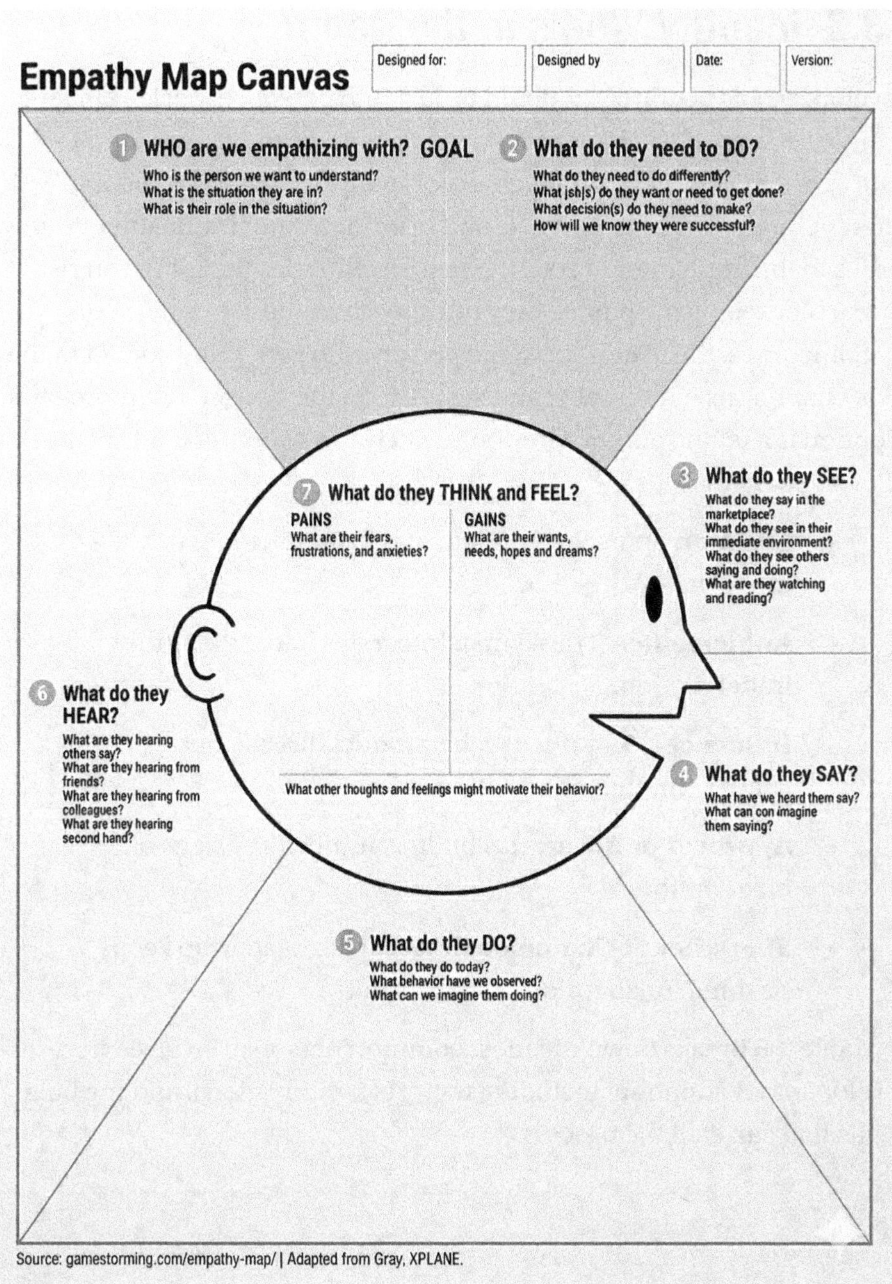

Figure 3-2. *Empathy Map Canvas*

3.3.3 Identify Who's in the Room

Developer tools are rarely adopted by just one person; especially in larger or more security-conscious organizations, buying and using a new tool is a team sport. Inside every ICP-aligned company, there are real people with different roles, levels of influence, and priorities. And if your strategy only speaks to the implementer (i.e., the person who tries the tool), you risk getting blocked by the people they need to convince.

Sometimes, the user is the same person who gets your product in the door, champions it internally, and signs off on the budget. But more often, adoption is a team sport, where you're likely to encounter a mix of the following personas:

- **Initiator**: Spots the problem and brings the tool to the team.

- **Implementer**: Tries it first, integrates it, runs into the initial friction.

- **Influencer**: May not use the product directly but shapes whether or how it's used.

- **Approver or Buyer**: Has budget authority or signs off on adoption.

- **Supporter or Champion**: Internal advocate who keeps pushing for adoption or expansion.

Table 3-6 breaks down the most common personas involved in developer tool adoption, including their role, motivations, and the pain points that can stall the process.

Table 3-6. *Common personas involved in developer tool adoption*

Persona	Role in Adoption	Motivators / Triggers	Common Pain Points
Initiator	Spots the problem or opportunity; brings your tool into the conversation	Wants to reduce toil, increase velocity, or solve a recurring pain	Needs a clear "why this, why now" story
User / Implementor	Uses or integrates the tool into their day-to-day workflows	Wants something reliable, understandable, well-documented	Friction in DX, unclear docs, edge-case failures
Influencer	Trusted voice in the org (staff+ engineer, tech lead, or architect)	Interested in architecture fit, long-term maintainability, alignment with internal standards	Needs a deep technical understanding and answers to "Will this scale with us?"
Approver / Buyer	Holds the budget or authority to greenlight the purchase	Cares about ROI, compliance, vendor risk, cost of switching	Will bounce if the business case isn't obvious, or if integration looks risky

Let's go back to our **Git commit signing tool** example. You might see this type of adoption sequence:

- A **DevOps engineer** (Initiator + Implementor) notices that unsigned commits could pose a risk in their CI/CD pipeline. They bring the tool in and try it locally.

- A **security architect** (Influencer) is looped in to assess how this fits with the org's broader identity strategy.

- The team's **engineering manager** (Approver) gets involved to evaluate budget, support, and rollout risk before approving widespread use.

If your content, documentation, or onboarding speaks only to the DevOps engineer, adoption might stall. If it focuses only on high-level security outcomes, the engineer might never try it. That's why understanding the room matters.

Once you understand who is involved, you can start to build for them. That doesn't mean you need a separate campaign for each role, but you do need to address their priorities, questions, and blockers across your content and DevRel strategy.

3.3.4 Uncover the Jobs to Be Done

Now that you've identified who's involved in adopting your product, the next step is understanding what each person is actually trying to accomplish. This is where the Jobs to Be Done framework becomes powerful. It shifts your focus from titles and roles to motivations and outcomes.

The Jobs to Be Done (JTBD) framework originated in the world of product and innovation strategy, most notably shaped by Clayton Christensen, a Harvard Business School professor best known for his work on disruptive innovation. The central idea behind JTBD is that people don't simply buy products or tools; they "hire" them to do a specific job. If the product does the job well, they keep using it. If it doesn't, they fire it and look for something else.

Traditional marketing personas often reduce people to titles or roles. JTBD gives you richer insight. It reflects what developers and decision-makers are actually trying to do. If someone's job is "I want to ship secure code without changing my current workflow," your job is to *show* how your tool does that.

Let's go back to our example of the Git commit signing tool and apply the JTBD approach to each key persona in the room:

Table 3-7. *Jobs to Be Done for key personas in developer tool adoption, showing their goals, priorities, and the content or resources that address them*

Persona	Job to Be Done	What They Care About	What You Might Create
Initiator	Identify gaps in the CI/CD pipeline and propose solutions	Fast fixes for urgent problems, respect from peers	"Why unsigned commits are a risk" blog post, Slack-ready explainer
Implementer	Set up the tool and verify that it works across environments	Clear docs, smooth onboarding, minimal surprises	Step-by-step tutorial, test repo, install script
Influencer	Ensure the solution fits broader security or compliance goals	Policy enforcement, traceability, standards alignment	Architecture diagrams, security overview, compliance one-pager
Approver	Decide whether the team should invest time and resources	Cost-benefit tradeoffs, team impact, rollout risk	ROI calculator, team enablement checklist, case study PDF
Supporter	Champion the tool internally and make adoption easier	Developer experience, peer confidence, credibility	Live demo talk, success story, internal Q&A deck

Table 3-7 maps the Jobs to Be Done for each key persona, showing what they care about and what content or resources will move them forward. Each of these jobs carries both a practical goal and an emotional trigger. The DevOps engineer wants to automate something securely, but they also want to be seen as competent. The engineering manager wants risk reduction, but also needs confidence that this isn't going to blow up in their backlog. The security architect wants to strengthen posture, but also needs to show traceability to leadership.

When you understand these jobs, your content becomes sharper. Your advocacy becomes more relevant. And your strategy becomes more effective. You stop writing vague blog posts and start producing the exact material that moves people through the adoption journey.

3.4 Finally, Understand the Team

One of the most common reasons developer advocacy teams struggle to prove their value is because they operate in isolation. They're building content, supporting communities, and speaking at events, but nobody outside the DevRel team really understands what they're doing or how it connects to the company's goals. Internally, DevRel is often misperceived as a team that travels, tweets, and runs the occasional workshop. Useful, maybe. But not essential.

That disconnect becomes dangerous in the kind of economic climate we're now in. The ZIRP (Zero Interest Rate Policy) era is over. Companies are being told to "get fit" and "do more with less." That translates into smaller teams, tighter budgets, and a renewed focus on outcomes that move the bottom line. It also means that in some organizations, entire DevRel teams are being downsized—or cut completely—because leadership doesn't see a clear return.

Before you commit to a strategy, you need to know what your developer advocacy team is already doing and how that connects to the activities of other relevant teams inside your company. When developer advocacy works in a vacuum, it becomes invisible. When it becomes a bridge between developers and the rest of the business, its value becomes undeniable.

Even if your team is doing great work, it won't be recognized unless it's aligned with something the company already values. How does your work support product goals, marketing campaigns, customer success metrics, or sales conversations? What teams rely on what you create? What internal priorities could your work accelerate?

3.4.1 Sync with Surrounding Teams

Start by asking

- What does marketing care about right now?

- What's sales trying to move?

- What's product struggling to prioritize?

- What queries are customer success frequently fielding?

Each of these departments has a wish list. Your work can support it—if you take the time to understand it. This doesn't mean you have to do everything. But you do need to identify which parts align with your team's purpose, and which efforts will generate the clearest lift across the business. The goal is to become the team everyone instinctively turns to for developer-related insights, feedback, and enablement—without needing to be reminded by leadership.

Marketing is focused on awareness, positioning, lead generation, and supporting the sales funnel. Their world runs on campaigns, launches, SEO rankings, and measurable conversions. They're asking: how do we get the right people to care about us? They may need technically accurate content to support a launch, an SEO boost on specific keywords, or case studies that show real-world use. You can surface developer questions and pain points that inform messaging and campaign focus or Collaborate early on go-to-market plans to bring a developer lens to positioning

Product teams are focused on building the right things, making the experience smoother, and gathering feedback to guide future work. They're asking: are we solving the right problems? And are developers happy with how we're doing it? They may need developer feedback on a beta feature, better examples for their docs, or early validation on a new workflow. If your company is product-led, your work might focus more on feedback loops and onboarding friction than lead generation. It's not just enough to answer questions on Stack Overflow that are related to your product. After all, Engineering, Technical Support, or Product could likely do that as well. But if you can spot patterns and trends throughout the tech industry while spending time engaging with your community on Stack Overflow, you're then able to bring your unique perspective back to the company. This information can then be used by Marketing to create additional content; Product to decide on the best way forward with a new feature; and even Sales to highlight new use cases during their calls with prospects.

Sales teams are focused on moving qualified leads through the pipeline and closing deals. They're asking: how do we convince the right people that our product is worth buying? They may need credible technical content to share during calls, competitive positioning support, or examples that help unstick a hesitant prospect. If your company is sales-led, one of your highest-leverage contributions might be internal sales enablement content—even if it doesn't drive SEO traffic. Your blog post doesn't have to go viral to be successful. If a technical guide you wrote helps close a six-figure deal, that's a win—whether it got five views or five thousand.

Customer Success teams are focused on onboarding, retention, and helping users realize the value they were promised. Their goal is simple: keep users happy, engaged, and successful—so they stay. They're asking: how do we help developers adopt our product effectively? How do we make sure they don't get stuck or give up? This team is often closest to real-world usage pain. They know where users drop off during onboarding, what features are hard to understand, and where documentation falls short. That makes them a goldmine for developer advocates. The feedback they surface can—and should—shape your strategy. They may need onboarding walkthroughs, live training content, or blog posts to fill recurring knowledge gaps. DevRel can help here by identifying those gaps early, producing supporting content, and making it easier for developers to succeed long before they reach a support ticket.

Some of the most valuable content I've ever created came directly from customer success feedback. I remember a time when customer success reported that some customers were curious about our stance on quantum computing and how we were preparing for that shift. So I wrote a piece to address that question. That blog post became one of our most shared internally. Our customer success team sent it to several key accounts. It helped unblock conversations, and one of those accounts expanded their usage and bought into a cross-sell offer on the spot.

3.4.2 Audit Your Current Dev Advocacy Initiatives

Now that you understand the goal of the company and that of other complementary teams, it's time to analyze current DevRel activities through that lens.

Take a step back and ask: what initiatives are currently active? What's in progress? What have we quietly abandoned? What's generating value, and what's draining effort without impact?

This kind of audit helps you establish a baseline. It gives you a grounded sense of your team's capacity, surface area, and blind spots. It also helps you figure out what to include in your strategy, what should be re-evaluated, and what should be let go entirely.

Step 1: List Every Current and Recent Initiative

Start by gathering everything your team has worked on in the last 3–6 months. Include the following:

- Active projects (content series, events, partnerships)
- Recurring responsibilities (supporting forums, managing a Discord, writing docs)
- Abandoned or paused experiments
- Anything taking regular time that isn't clearly tracked

You're looking for the full picture, not just what's in the roadmap doc. Dig through Slack threads, Notion pages, internal team calendars—whatever it takes.

Step 2: For Each Initiative, Ask the Right Questions

Go down the list, one initiative at a time, and ask

- What was the goal of this work?
- Is the initiative still active or running passively?
- What signals (if any) show it's working?
- What known issues or blockers exist?
- Does anyone own this initiative? Should they?
- If this disappeared tomorrow, who would notice?

These questions help you separate energy from impact. They also highlight where effort is leaking due to unclear ownership or forgotten intent.

Step 3: Assess Strategic Fit

Once you've asked the operational questions, add a layer of strategic thinking. For each initiative, consider:

- Does this align with the company's current goals?

- Does it support a specific developer segment or ICP?

- Is this helping us grow, retain, or support the right users?

- Is the effort-to-impact ratio sustainable?

You don't need perfect answers. You need directional clarity. This exercise gives you the language to make decisions as a team—and a filter to use when new ideas come up.

Step 4: Decide What to Keep

When the audit is complete, share it with the team (and relevant stakeholders). Then, as a team, categorize the initiatives:

- **Double down**: High impact, aligned with strategy

- **Revise or relaunch**: Promising, but needs attention

- **Pause or archive**: No longer aligned or worth the effort

Instead of reacting or carrying legacy work forward by default, you're now choosing what to prioritize, and why.

Summary: Bring It All Together

You've now laid the groundwork for a developer advocacy strategy that's not only thoughtful, but aligned. You've looked closely at the company you're working within, its goals, growth stage, business model, and position in the market. You've studied the product in detail, from what it actually does to how it fits into the stack, who it competes with, and where it shines or stumbles. You've clarified your target developer audience, built out your segmentation, and defined your ideal customer profile. You've mapped out the roles that matter in adoption, and you've started to think about the jobs they're trying to get done—not just what they say they want, but what they're really trying to accomplish.

Finally, you've taken stock of your own team. You've audited what's already in motion, and you've looked outward to understand how your work connects—or could connect—to marketing, product, customer support, and sales.

This is the kind of foundational work that separates teams that spin their wheels from teams that make real impact.

In the next chapter, you'll take everything you've uncovered—about the company, the product, the audience, and your team—and start to turn it into a concrete developer advocacy plan. You'll learn how to choose the right content medium to focus on, how to define goals that actually map to business outcomes, and how to measure the value you're creating over time.

CHAPTER 4

Crafting Your Developer Advocacy Strategy

Your developer advocacy strategy starts with clarity. If you followed the framework from Chapter 3, you should already have the raw material: you've mapped your company's goals, understood the product's strengths and friction points, identified your target developer segments, and audited your team's current activities. You also know what other departments are working toward, and where you as a developer advocate fit in.

In this chapter, we'll take those insights and turn them into a focused strategy with clear priorities, defined objectives, and measurable outcomes. You'll learn how to set a strategic focus, define OKRs that align with it, pick your strategic bets, and say no to distractions.

4.1 Choose Your Strategic Bets and Define Your OKRs

Once you understand your company's goals, your product's maturity stage, and what developers need most, the next step is to define how Developer

L. Ikechukwu, *A Friendly Guide to Developer Advocacy*, Friendly Guides to Technology, https://doi.org/10.1007/979-8-8688-2462-3_4

Advocacy will contribute. That begins with choosing your strategic bets and defining OKRs, which together form the foundation of your strategic focus.

This process is best approached from the bottom up:

1. Choose high-leverage activities (your strategic bets) based on your company's goals and the developer journey.

2. Define OKRs that map to those activities and clarify what success looks like.

3. Use both to articulate a focused strategy statement; a single sentence that ties DevRel's efforts back to what the company is trying to achieve.

Let's clarify each step.

Your strategic bets are the high-leverage activities you'll prioritize. These are the initiatives, programs, or deliverables in the form of content formats you believe will most effectively advance your company's goals through developer engagement.

Every content format has trade-offs. A blog post is easier to SEO but harder to embed into a developer's workflow. A video can be more engaging but harder to skim. Choose the one that aligns with the job to be done and your company and product's maturity stage.

Your OKRs (Objectives and Key Results) define what success looks like and how you'll measure it. An objective is the outcome you want. An objective is actionable, inspirational, and aspirational. It starts with a verb: to drive, expand, advance, improve, etc.

The key results are how you'll track progress toward it, including clear timelines and measurable goals, for example, meet with 20 developers to get feedback about API usage to shape product direction by end of Q3. Here, meeting 20 developers is the measurable goal. It is trackable. "End of Q3" is the timeline.

Your strategic focus is the final synthesis. It connects the company's goal with the outcomes DevRel is uniquely positioned to influence. You can use this template: Because the company is trying to *[company goal]*, DevRel or I will *[how you'll help achieve it]*.

Why is this bottom-up approach helpful?

Because as with any role that includes a lot of responsibilities and touchpoints, you'll quickly discover there's more than enough work to go round. This is true when you're the only person in DevRel, but even in teams of ten or more, this challenge remains. The work is vast and the possibilities endless.

To set priorities wisely, you must first understand the phase your company is in. For instance, you might be tempted to prioritize sponsorship events, but if the business is still pre-product-market-fit, those may not deliver the performance you need at the top of the funnel. At that point, having documentation and sample code to help prospective customers get started, or demos to show what the product makes possible and as a sales-enablement tool are more important and urgent.

Or perhaps you're eager to automate user journeys through email campaigns, but if the developer onboarding experience is still broken, that effort may be premature.

In DevRel, there are often more things you'll need to delay than do immediately. And that's okay. Focus now. Do more later.

Since the first step in defining your strategy is picking your strategic bets, it helps to have a framework for comparing the many activities Developer Relations could take on.

Table 4-1 was inspired by Phil Leggetter's NESMO AAARRRP Google Sheet, first presented at DevRelCon London 2016. It can be used as a practical reference for deciding which activities to prioritize or which bets to make based on your company's goals and product maturity. It maps common DevRel activities to the AAARRP funnel stages discussed in Chapter 3 and assigns each a priority rating.

The priority ratings are about timing, company needs, and product maturity.

- **Must-have**: Foundational activities that nearly every startup should prioritize first. They form the basic scaffolding for developer success, especially when the company is early-stage and still proving product–market fit.

- **High priority**: High-leverage activities that accelerate adoption and retention once the must-haves are in place. These tend to suit companies that have moved beyond the scrappy startup phase and are entering early growth.

- **Medium priority**: Activities that become most valuable at the growth or expansion stage, when the product is more stable and the company is scaling developer engagement.

- **Low priority**: Activities that typically belong in a maturity stage, when DevRel programs are well-resourced and can afford to expand into complementary or experimental initiatives.

Table 4-1. *Developer Relations activity matrix mapping common DevRel initiatives to AAARRRP funnel stages and their relative priority based on company maturity and goals*

Activity	Awareness	Acquisition	Activation	Retention	Revenue	Referral	Product	Priority
Docs -> Product Guides			x	x	x		x	Must Have
Docs -> References			x	x	x		x	Must Have
Docs -> Quick starts			x	x	x		x	Must Have
Docs -> Tutorials	x		x	x	x		x	High
Libraries			x	x	x		x	High
Sample Apps / Use cases	x	x	x	x		x	x	High
Blog -> Tutorials	x	x	x	x		x		Medium
Blog -> Hacks	x	x		x		x		Medium
Blog -> Thought Leadership	x			x		x		Low
Webinars	x		x	x		x		Medium
Events -> Hackathons	x	x	x				x	Medium
Events -> Sponsorship	x							Medium
Events -> Booths	x	x						Low
Talks / Workshops -> Conferences	x	x						Medium
Talks / Meetups	x	x						High
Support -> Tickets			x	x		x		Must Have
Support -> Third-party forums syndication & listening	x		x	x		x	x	Medium
Support -> Owned community forums			x	x		x	x	High
Pre-Sales -> Discussions			x	x	x	x	x	Medium
Pre-Sales -> Integration			x	x	x	x		Medium
Alpha/Beta Programmes			x	x			x	Medium
Office Hours			x	x			x	Medium
Capture Feedback				x			x	Medium
Help company recruitment	x							Medium
Ambassador programs				x	x	x		Low
Podcast and streaming	x	x				x		Medium
SDK / Sandboxes		x		x	x			Must Have
Certification / Training Program				x		x		Low
Social media content (video / text)	x	x				x		Medium

Now, to illustrate the process of picking strategic bets, OKRS, and a strategic focus in action, let's walk through four company scenarios and see how each one shapes the strategic bets, OKRs, and strategic focus statement:

- You're working at an early-stage company. The company's primary goal for the year is to increase user base by 30%, and achieve a 20% increase in annual recurring revenue.

- You're working at a scale-up company entering a new phase of growth, intending to expand into new markets (e.g., EMEA).

- You're working at a sales-led company whose goal for the quarter is to acquire five new enterprise customers.

- You're working at a product-led company with an established user base, whose goal is to increase developer retention (i.e., reduce churn) and raise awareness and usage of the open-source offering.

1. ***You're working at an early-stage company whose primary goal for the year is to increase the user base by 30% and achieve a 20% increase in annual recurring revenue.***

   Start by interpreting what this goal really means for DevRel.

   This is about adoption. That means your work needs to influence **Acquisition**, **Activation**, **Retention**, and **Revenue** and maybe Awareness in the AAARRRP framework.

   So how do you contribute?

   You look at what's blocking developers from adopting. Maybe it's poor docs. Maybe it's a confusing "Hello World." Maybe no one even knows your product exists. These insights point you to the activities that will create the most impact.

Assuming that the problem isn't that no one knows that your product exists. Traffic is healthy, but not much of that traffic signs up; maybe because the use cases aren't immediately clear or the messaging is wrong. And that when the traffic does sign up, only a few make it past setting up, maybe because onboarding friction is high. In that case, the problem might be that developers don't immediately see the product's use cases or value or it doesn't serve them in the way they expect.

Referencing Table 4-1, we look at the priority table for higher-priority activities that influence the stages of the AAARRRP framework we want to affect.

Based on that, you might define OKRs like these:

Objective A: Improve onboarding to support user growth.

- **KR1:** Publish three new SEO-optimized "Hello World" tutorials in both video and blog formats that demonstrate practical use cases for the top three developer frameworks (e.g., React, Django, and Node) by the end of Q3.

- **KR2**: Create and promote 2 starter repos with pre-configured environments that reduce setup time by end of Q3.

- **KR3:** Run 5 onboarding walkthrough interviews to identify friction points and publish a report of findings by Q4.

Objective B: Improve feedback loop with Product to reduce developer churn.

- **KR1**: Surface 10 actionable pieces of feedback to Product by end of Q3.

- **KR2**: Close the loop by publishing at least 5 "you asked, we built" content pieces by end of Q4.

Objective C: Reduce friction in support by scaling self-serve help.

- **KR1**: Convert 50% of repetitive support questions into documentation by end of Q3.

2. ***You're working at a scale-up company entering a new phase of growth and the company's primary goal for the quarter is to expand into new markets (e.g., EMEA).***

This goal is about **market expansion**. For DevRel, this often maps to the **Awareness**, **Acquisition**, and **Activation** growth stages, and to the **Discover**, **Evaluate**, and **Scale** stages in the developer journey.

Your goal is to help developers in new markets find your product, understand its relevance, and reach their first success quickly, all while building trust and credibility within the region.

So what should you prioritize?

From our template, high-leverage activities for this kind of growth include

When we look at Table 4-1, we see that certain activities and content types are consistently ranked high priority in these stages:

- **Discover**: Blog content, developer hubs, social media, content syndication, developer-focused marketing, and referral programs

- **Evaluate**: Strong documentation, landing pages, FAQs, and case studies

- **Scale**: Feedback programs, access to your product roadmap, and participation in beta testing groups

These insights from Table 4-1 are useful, but they're not prescriptive. For example, some Discover-stage activities like podcast features or regional case studies may not be labeled "high priority" in the table, but they can be powerful tools for building trust in a new market, especially when you're operating as a scale-up trying to earn credibility quickly. The table is not a rulebook. It is a tool. The right activities for your team will always depend on your company's growth stage, product maturity, and the specific needs of your developer audience.

With that in mind, here's how this strategic focus might translate into OKRs:

Objective A: Increase product visibility and regional trust in EMEA.

- **KR1**: Sponsor or speak at 3 regional developer events or podcasts by Q4.

- **KR2**: Launch a regional ambassador or community chapter program in at least two key cities by end of Q4.

- **KR3**: Publish two case studies featuring EMEA-based customers by end of Q4.

Objective B: Improve onboarding experience for EMEA developers.

- **KR1**: Localize and create region-specific key landing pages to address local infrastructure needs, compliance expectations, and developer norms by the middle of Q4.

Strategic bets like these should reflect your unique context. Use the framework I've shared to spark ideas, weigh trade-offs, and defend your choices with confidence, but let your product, audience, and business goals lead the way.

Once you've defined your strategic bets and written your OKRs, it's time to crystallize the work into a strategy statement. This is the sentence you'll return to when you're explaining your team's role or defending your priorities. Use the formula:

Because the company is trying to *[company goal]*,
this quarter DevRel will *[how you'll help achieve it]*.

So for the early-stage company above, you might say.

Because the company is trying to grow its user base and revenue, this quarter DevRel will focus on driving adoption by removing onboarding blockers, improving product learning resources, and surfacing user feedback to guide product development.

For the scale-up example:

Because the company is expanding into new markets, this quarter DevRel will focus on accelerating regional adoption by building local trust, supporting tailored onboarding experiences, and cultivating developer community presence across key regions.

Now it's your turn. For the remaining two company scenarios, the sales-led and product-led, can you take a stab at defining strategic bets, OKRs, and finally a strategic statement for them?

Summary

OKRs create focus, alignment, and accountability. They also give stakeholders a clear picture of what DevRel is prioritizing and why.

Strong Key Results should include clear timelines. Otherwise, they risk being vague aspirations instead of measurable commitments. The timeline grounds each objective in urgency and accountability, and allows teams to track progress in meaningful review cycles, whether quarterly, biannually, or annually.

You don't need many. Most teams do best with two to four OKRs per quarter or half-year. Each objective should have two to three key results.

In the next chapter, we'll explore how to define success beyond OKRs, through KPIs, metrics, and qualitative indicators. You'll also see how to bring all of this together into a strategy template you can use to align your team and communicate your plan internally.

By the end of the next chapter, you'll have a complete, presentable developer advocacy strategy.

CHAPTER 5

Executing Your Strategy (Best Practices for Developer-Focused Content and Programs)

Chapter 4 walked you through how to define your strategic focus and choose your strategic bets. Whether you decided to fix documentation, build sample apps, give talks, run webinars, ship tutorials, or launch community programs, those are all forms of content. Content reigns supreme. The nuance lies in what content, for whom, with what intention, and with 5-1: what distribution strategy.

This chapter is your guide to executing those different strategic bets or content formats well. We'll break down the major content types and show you how to make the most out of each, so you're not just producing content, but creating assets that move developers and drive meaningful outcomes.

© Linda Ikechukwu 2026

L. Ikechukwu, *A Friendly Guide to Developer Advocacy*, Friendly Guides to Technology, https://doi.org/10.1007/979-8-8688-2462-3_5

You'll also learn how to scale your impact with AI tools, improve your workflow without compromising quality, distribute your work more effectively, and build repeatable systems that help you stay consistent without burning out.

5.1 What Makes Developer Content Actually Work?

Good developer content is not just accurate or well-written. It's useful, discoverable, and designed to reduce friction. Developers are busy. They are problem-solving. If your content helps them do that faster or better, they will value it, even if the presentation isn't perfect.

Here's what separates great developer content from everything else:

5.1.1 It Solves a Real Problem

Developers don't care about what your product does. They care about what your product lets them do. The best content doesn't just describe features. It helps developers accomplish something they already care about. It answers their questions. It makes their lives easier. It gets them unblocked.

When you lead with features, you're looking inward—talking about what you've built. That's fine for internal demos. But when you're speaking to developers, start with their perspective. What problem are they trying to solve? What outcome are they chasing? Then show them how your product gets them there.

Here's what our product can do vs. here's what our product can do for you sound similar, but they're miles apart in intent.

Instead of "How to use our API with a 1-second response time," try

- "How to build a Slackbot that texts you when your CI pipeline fails"

- "How to sync Airtable and Notion in 5 minutes using X API"

Samuel Hulick (`https://www.samuelhulick.com/`) captured this perfectly with his Super Mario analogy, illustrated in Figure 5-1. Mario doesn't care about the flower. He cares that the flower lets him shoot fireballs.

Figure 5-1. *The Super Mario analogy by Samuel Hulick illustrating that users don't care about your product itself but about what it enables them to do*

People don't buy products; they buy better versions of themselves. When you're trying to win customers, are you listing the attributes of the flower or describing how awesome it is to throw fireballs?

Start with the problem, not the product. Tell them how it actually improves their life.

5.1.2 It's Written for a Specific Stage of the Developer Journey

Great content meets the developer where they are—technically, contextually, and emotionally. It respects their time, their level of experience, and the problem they're trying to solve right now. Your job is to calibrate your content to that context.

Don't write advanced migration guides for someone still figuring out how to authenticate their first request. Don't explain what an API is to an architect evaluating your product for a large-scale integration. You need to meet developers where they are, not where you wish they were.

That means two things:

First, content should be matched to a clear stage in the developer journey. A beginner just discovering your product needs something very different from a senior engineer evaluating it for a migration. Awareness-stage developers benefit from broad, conceptual overviews or inspirational demos. Evaluation-stage developers want side-by-side comparisons, code samples, and clear docs. Post-adoption developers care about advanced use cases, troubleshooting, and what's coming next. When you don't tailor content to these stages, it either confuses or bores the reader, and wastes your effort.

Table 5-1 maps each stage of the developer journey against experience level and the content types most likely to land.

Table 5-1. *Content Strategy Matrix aligning developer journey stages
with experience levels and recommended content types to ensure
relevance and impact*

Content Strategy Matrix

Developer Journey Stage	Experience Level	Content Type
Discover	Beginner	Intro blog posts, explainer videos
Discover	Experienced	Talks, ecosystem comparisons
Evaluate	Beginner	Getting started guides, tutorials
Evaluate	Experienced	API comparisons, security docs
Learn	Beginner	FAQs, walkthroughs
Learn	Experienced	Advanced use cases, architecture guides
Build	Beginner	Starter repos, quickstarts
Build	Experienced	Migration guides, SDK integrations
Scale	Beginner	Community programs, product update summaries
Scale	Experienced	Roadmap briefings, changelogs

Second, it should consider experience level. Use empathy to calibrate
tone, pacing, and assumed knowledge. Don't waste time on API basics
when writing for staff engineers. Don't skip foundational concepts when
writing for beginners. This doesn't mean dumbing things down. It means
being thoughtful about what your reader already knows, and what they
need next.

The best developer content signals who it's for. It acknowledges
different knowledge levels by layering information and makes space for
advanced learning without overcomplicating the basics. It offers

- Entry points for new users and learners

- Deeper technical details for experienced users

- Advanced use cases and optimizations for experts

Twilio's documentation does this exceptionally well, offering quick starts for beginners alongside detailed API references and more advanced tutorials for complex implementation scenarios.

Not every piece needs to serve everyone, but your library should make it clear who each piece is helping and how.

5.1.3 It's Skimmable and Easy to Follow

Structure matters. Developers are rarely reading for leisure and don't always read top to bottom. They're in the middle of something. They're scanning. They're jumping between tabs.

They want clear headings, copy-pasteable code, and a way to check that they're doing it right.

That means

- Showing expected outputs so they know it's working

- Warning about common errors and how to fix them

- Breaking steps into chunks

- Using real, runnable code—not just pseudocode

- Prioritizing whitespace, bullets, and subheadings over
  dense text

Make it easy to jump around. Include summaries up top. Think of content as a product whose job is to reduce time-to-success.

5.2 Format-Specific Best Practices

You've picked your strategic bets. You've been told general rules on how to make engaging developer content. Now it's time to learn how to execute them individually well.

This section walks through the most common content formats Developer Advocates create and how to approach each one with clarity, intention, and impact.

5.2.1 Webinars and Online Events

Online events are one of the most scalable tools in your developer relations toolkit. With the right approach, a single session can reach hundreds or thousands of developers in real time, then continue creating value for months through recordings, blog posts, and follow-up resources.

But great online events don't happen by accident. They're the result of thoughtful planning, careful facilitation, and strong community instincts. Most importantly, they need to be designed for engagement, not just delivery.

Webinars and online meetups shine when you're trying to reach developers at scale, especially across time zones. They work well for showcasing new features, demonstrating integrations, teaching best practices, answering community questions, or bringing in partners for joint sessions. They're also one of the most cost-effective ways to build community touchpoints because there are no flights, venue bookings, or travel budgets required.

How to Do Webinars Well

We'll break this into four phases: conception, preparation, execution, and wrap-up.

Conception: Design Your Event to Scale, Not Just to Present

Good webinars or online events solve a real problem. They are useful, timely, and relevant to developers' goals. That's how you get people interested in attending.

- **Start by listening**: If you don't know what to speak about, start by listening. What are developers struggling with in your community? What new capability are people curious about? What's being asked over and over again in your support forums or Discord? Build your ideas around those signals.

- **Consider pre-recording your presentation**: If you're going to be presenting sensitive demos or early-stage features, you should probably consider recording that section of the presentation. This ensures that things run smoothly, avoids awkward technical delays, and gives speakers a chance to polish their message. You can still run a live Q&A afterward to retain that sense of interactivity.

- **Consider time zones**: If your developer audience is global, consider alternating times across regions or running two versions of the same talk. Some teams even run "follow the sun" webinars with handoffs across regions.

- **Don't overstuff the agenda**: A single focused topic beats an overly broad one. For awareness events, aim for under 60 minutes. For hands-on workshops, you can stretch to 90 minutes, but you'll need to design the experience carefully using simple setup instructions, easy-to-follow demos, and clear pacing. Avoid making attendees jump between five tools before they've written a single line of code.

Preparation: Promote and Rehearse Heavily

If no one shows up to your webinar, then you've probably failed before you even started. Don't treat promotion as an afterthought. Start 2 to 3 weeks in advance. Share your event in your newsletter, your community Slack or Discord, promote and maybe run ads on LinkedIn and other relevant platforms, ask your co-workers to share with their own network too.

Drive engagement before the event. One tactic that works well is inviting people to submit questions ahead of time. This has two benefits: first, it gives you backup material in case the live audience is quiet. Second, it tells you what your audience cares about most, so you can tailor your presentation accordingly.

You'll also want to do at least one dry run with your speakers. If they're not experienced with virtual presentations, this is essential. Test the platform. Make sure they know how to share their screen, toggle audio, and interact with the chat. Check lighting, sound, background, and posture. Walk through transitions and timing. If you're using live captioning, test that too.

Assign a host or moderator to every event. Ideally, this isn't the same person as the presenter. The host can introduce the speaker, manage logistics, handle Q&A, and keep the audience engaged. Their presence makes the session feel more polished and conversational, rather than one-way and transactional.

Execution: Deliver a Human, High-Quality Experience

When it's time to go live, your job is to make the event feel alive. A few seconds of warmth at the start can make a world of difference. Greet the audience. Ask where they're joining from. Mention a few names from the chat. This reminds people that they're not just watching a video—they're part of something happening in real time.

Use two facilitators if you can: one person to present, the other to moderate and support the flow. The moderator can queue up questions, post links to resources, and help guide the discussion. If you're demoing code, have the moderator drop the GitHub link in chat right before you start.

Make sure your visuals are designed for online delivery. Slides should have large, readable text. Avoid dense bullet lists. Keep high-contrast colors and clean layouts. If you're coding live, zoom in your editor and highlight what matters.

Talk to the camera as if you're speaking to a friend. Eye contact and facial expression go a long way. Sit up straight. Emote with your voice. If you mess up, smile and keep going. You're human. That's a good thing.

Record the session automatically. Tools like Crowdcast, Zoom, and Google Meet offer auto-recording features so you don't forget. This is your content archive in the making.

Wrap-up: Extend the Life of Your Event

Your online event doesn't end when you hit "End Meeting." That's just phase one. Next comes the part where you maximize the value of what you've created.

- **Publish the recording**: Upload to YouTube or another searchable platform. Add timestamps for sections or questions.

- **Repurpose the content**: Turn the talk into a blog post, Twitter thread, or Reddit summary, a LinkedIn summary, maybe even a podcast or TikTok clip. Answer leftover Q&A in a follow-up post.

- **Send a thank-you email**: Include the recording, slides, answers to any unanswered questions, links to further learning or next steps and a feedback form. Let people know what's coming next. Don't be afraid to reshare the recording weeks later, especially if it's evergreen. A solid technical talk is just as valuable three months after it aired.

- **Use the momentum**: Point attendees to your next event or a related tutorial. Invite them to join your community or sign up for product updates.

5.2.2 Talks

Talks are powerful for driving awareness and acquisition in the developer journey, while offering something most other formats cannot: immediate, in-person feedback. Imagine delivering a session on how to use your API to solve a common developer pain point, then seeing in real time which parts resonate, which create confusion, and which spark curiosity. You walk away with new visibility for your product and a deeper understanding of how your audience thinks and reacts.

Joe Nash, one of GitHub's early developer advocates, shared how the company focused on speaking at as many local meetups and grassroots events as possible to build recognition. In his first three months, he spoke at 39 local events, which quickly created awareness and established GitHub's name in early developer communities. Those appearances put GitHub in the rooms where developers were already gathering, building relationships and credibility one audience at a time.

Talks work especially well for products that are free or freemium, student-friendly, or easy for solo developers to experiment with. Netlify, for example, is ideal for local developer and student meetups because anyone can use it to quickly host a website without complex setup. When your product fits this profile, consistent local speaking can accelerate adoption and build trust in ways that no blog post or video can match, because people remember people, not just companies.

If your product is harder to get started with, isn't relevant to your local developer communities, or you live in a city without many of these communities, you may get more value by first investing in scalable formats such as documentation, tutorials, and videos.

How to Do Talks Well

I have spoken at over 40 conferences across four continents (Africa, Asia, North America, and Europe), so I know a thing or two about giving talks.

Pick the Right Conferences

Not all conferences or speaking opportunities will bring the same return for your time and budget. The best events for developer advocates strike a balance between value for the company, relevance to your audience, and opportunities to receive feedback.

Speaking is also an investment in yourself. Some events give you access to peers, potential collaborators, and industry leaders you wouldn't otherwise meet. Others might be career milestones that boost your credibility in your space. When personal growth and company goals align, you've found a sweet spot.

- **Start with your product and audience fit**: The first and most important filter is the audience. Does the event attract the type of developer your product is built for. Conferences where your audience is already seeking solutions in your product's space are far more likely to lead to meaningful adoption.

For example, if you work on a CI/CD tool like CircleCI, DevOps-focused conferences such as DevOpsDays or All Day DevOps are better investments than a broad, general-tech conference. Smaller, niche events may draw fewer attendees but often produce higher engagement and better conversion rates, especially when the audience is tightly aligned with your product.

If you're not sure where your ideal audience gathers, try using ChatGPT or another AI tool to identify potential events. For example: *Here is my ideal developer persona: {describe your ICP, role, industry, location, and key problems they face}. Suggest 15 conferences, meetups, or events where this audience is likely to gather, and indicate which are local, regional, and global.*

— **Consider your company's strategic priorities**: Are you targeting enterprise adoption, mid-market developers, or indie developers? An enterprise security product will get more value from speaking at industry-specific summits and closed-door CIO events than from university hackathons. Conversely, an indie-friendly platform like Replit or Netlify will thrive at hackathons, student-run meetups, and open-source conferences, where experimentation is part of the culture. A talk with 200 people in the room closely aligned with your buyer persona is better than a large broad-based room.

— **Start local before you go global.** Speaking at local meetups and regional conferences helps you refine your talk, build relationships with community organizers, and test which messages resonate before investing in travel and sponsorship for international events. As Joe Nash's GitHub example shows, saturating local events can build powerful grassroots momentum. Once you've honed your message and built a track record of engaging talks, you'll be better prepared to stand out on bigger stages.

You also need to factor in the true cost of speaking. Travel, preparation time, and opportunity cost add up quickly. Will the event cover travel and accommodation? If not, can your company justify the spend based on expected impact? Will the prep work take focus away from higher-leverage activities? When budgets are tight, focus on local and regional opportunities to keep costs manageable.

— **Think beyond the talk itself:** If you are investing in travel, maximize the value of the trip. Consider if the conference offers session recordings, speaker interviews, or post-event content promotion, extending your reach long after the event. These assets can be repurposed in blog posts, newsletters, and social media. Also consider if the conferences can also serve as a strategic intelligence opportunity to observe competitors and other ecosystem players, learn from their positioning, and even open doors to networking and future collaborations.

Choose a Talk Topic

Once you've identified the right conferences or meetups to target, the next question is: what will you talk about? A great topic aligns your expertise, your company's goals, and the audience's needs. It also creates space for curiosity, discussion, and follow-up.

Start with the developer's point of view. Think about the problems they are actively trying to solve, the trends they are following, and the challenges that frustrate them. For example, if you're representing a deployment platform like Netlify, you could speak about "Deploying Your

First Jamstack Site in Minutes" at a student hackathon, because it solves a real pain point for people experimenting with web projects and fits the event's rapid-prototyping energy.

Tie the topic to your company's goals, but avoid turning it into a product pitch. The most effective DevRel talks demonstrate expertise and build trust, showing developers how to solve a problem in a way that naturally positions your product as part of the solution. A talk on "Securing APIs with OAuth 2.0" can be just as valuable to your company as a talk explicitly mentioning your API gateway, if it attracts the right audience and positions you as a trusted resource.

Draw from your direct experience. Case studies, "lessons learned" stories, and behind-the-scenes walkthroughs resonate because they are grounded in reality. As a developer advocate, you have unique insight into both the developer perspective and your product's internals—use that to tell a story only you can tell.

Whatever your talk is, make sure that it educates and inspires. That's the priority.

Look for inspiration in your daily work:

- Questions developers ask you repeatedly in support channels or office hours.

- Blog posts or tutorials you've written that sparked strong engagement.

- Features your team recently shipped that solve a clear developer problem.

- Interesting technical challenges you've overcome that others are likely to face.

Tailor the topic to the event's audience. A conference for senior engineers may expect deeper technical dives, while a student meetup might value quick wins and approachable examples. If you're not sure, review past talks from the same event to understand their style, technical depth, and recurring themes.

Finally, think about the talk's "sticky" element—the one idea or insight you want the audience to remember a week later. Talks that try to cover too much risk leaving the audience with nothing concrete to act on. Center your talk around that one memorable takeaway, and build the rest of the content to support it.

Prepare Your Talk Abstract

Most conferences will require you to submit an outline before you can be accepted as a speaker. Your abstract is a promise to the audience about what they will learn from your talk. It is also your sales pitch to the conference organizers, convincing them that your session will be a valuable addition to their lineup.

The first step is to ensure your talk aligns with the conference theme and target audience. Avoid abstracts that read like a sales deck. If your product appears in the talk, frame it in terms of the problem it solves and the lessons learned from using it, not as a commercial.

A strong abstract answers four questions, in this order:

1. What is this talk about?
    Summarize the topic in a single, clear statement. This is your hook and the reason someone will read further. Don't do too much. Talks that try to cover too much risk overwhelming the audience and diluting the message.

2. Why is this topic important?
    Identify the pain point, gap, or challenge that makes this worth discussing. Make the stakes clear so that the audience understands why it matters.

3. What is your solution or unique perspective?
    Offer a high-level suggestion or approach, and explain how your view is distinctive. Avoid going into too much detail, as the talk itself is where you will unpack the specifics.

4. Who is this talk for, and what will they learn?
    Specify the intended audience and list the practical,
    actionable takeaways. A great talk leaves attendees
    smarter and equipped to act. This is especially
    important when submitting to conferences with
    diverse audiences and multiple tracks.

If you struggle to answer these questions, try developing the talk as a blog post first. Even if your submission is rejected, you will have a polished piece of content ready to publish.

For example, here is one of my abstracts which has been accepted at several conferences:

> *Bring development closer to production with valid HTTPS certificates*

Dev/prod parity is one of the major rules of software engineering. With that in mind, if almost all production web pages now load via HTTPS, why is it that almost no one uses HTTPS in development? The traditional process of provisioning certificates to local environments is difficult. This is a problem because when development does not match production, bad things happen. Join me in this talk to learn how to use Smallstep's step-ca, an open-source Let's Encrypt equivalent, to automate certificate issuance in your development environments with just four commands.

Why this works:

- **Hook**: "Dev/prod parity is one of the major rules of software engineering."

- **Problem**: "If almost all production web pages now load via HTTPS, why is it that almost no one uses HTTPS in development?"

- **Empathy and cause**: "The traditional process… is difficult. This is a problem because when development does not match production, bad things happen."

- **Solution and takeaway**: "Join me in this talk to learn how to use Smallstep's step-ca to automate certificate issuance in your development environments with just four commands."

A well-crafted abstract gives reviewers confidence in your ability to engage the audience and deliver value. It also helps potential attendees self-select into your session, ensuring the right people are in the room.

Prepping and Delivering Your Talk

Once your talk is accepted, the real work begins. Your goal is to transform the promise in your abstract into a presentation that delivers clear value to your audience while keeping their attention from start to finish.

There are so many resources and YouTube videos on the art of public speaking, and I think you should dig deeper and try different styles till you find what works for you. However, as someone who has spoken at over 40 conferences across 4 continents, here are a few quick tips I can share:

- **Use a narrative arc**: Think of your talk as a story with a beginning, middle, and end. A logical flow helps your audience follow along without losing context.

  - **Beginning**: Set the stage, explain the problem, and connect with your audience's experiences. Your opening sets the tone for the entire talk. Begin by briefly introducing yourself and immediately framing the problem or opportunity your talk addresses. Remind the audience what they will gain from listening. This reinforces the "what's in it for me" factor and encourages them to stay engaged.

106

- **Middle**: Present your solution, insights, or lessons learned. Break it into logical sections to make it digestible.

- **End**: Summarize key points, give clear next steps or actions, and invite continued engagement.

- **Your slides should support your talk, not distract**: Slides are a visual aid, not a script. Use them to highlight key points, show diagrams, and provide examples. Keep text minimal so the audience listens to you rather than reading the screen. When showing code, enlarge the font and highlight the important lines. If your code sample is too long to fit legibly, split it across slides or show on the relevant sections.

  Strong visuals also help and make your talk more memorable. These could be architecture diagrams, process flows, test results, or screenshots from your product in action. Use more visuals than words, if possible. If you have data, present it in clear, readable charts.

- **Decide on demos and live coding carefully**: My personal stance is never to do live coding if you can help it. Demos can be engaging, but they introduce risk. If you choose to do live coding, prepare for common pitfalls: Internet outages, typos, and unexpected errors. Have a backup plan, such as a recorded screencast of the demo, so you can continue smoothly if something goes wrong.

- **Use QR codes instead of links**: Use QR codes to provide attendees with a way to access your slides, resources, and related materials. Not only does this make it easier for your audience to follow up, but many link shorteners provide analytics you can share internally as evidence of engagement.

- **Rehearse in realistic conditions**: Goes without saying that you should practice your talk over and over again before the D-day. The difference between a great talk and a terrible one is an unrehearsed speaker. Practice with the exact setup you will use during the event: your microphone, camera, and lighting for virtual talks, or standing and projecting your voice for in-person talks. Track your timing carefully. Presenting live often speeds up your delivery, so aim to finish slightly under the allotted time during practice. Include checkpoints in your outline for where you should be at specific times. If you find yourself ahead of schedule during the talk, expand on examples or take a few questions. If you are running long, skip less critical points and move toward your conclusion.

- **Plan your Q&A strategy**: If the event includes Q&A, decide how you will handle it. As a rule of thumb, I prefer to take questions only at the end of the talk and not in-between, to avoid cutting my flow short. Repeat each question before answering so the entire room and the recording can hear it. If you do not know the answer, it is better to say so and offer to follow up than to speculate. Bring a clear way for attendees to reach you after the talk.

- **Stay calm and be yourself:** Nerves can make you speak too quickly, while overcompensating can make you sound flat. Focus on enunciating your words and maintaining a steady rhythm. If you are speaking to an international audience, remember that not everyone may be a native speaker of your language, so clarity matters more than speed.

If presenting in person, make eye contact with different sections of the room. If virtual, look into the camera to create the feeling of direct connection. Use open body language, smile when appropriate, and let your enthusiasm for the topic show.

Also remember to pause. Pausing briefly after a key point gives the audience a moment to absorb it. It also allows you to breathe, reset, and avoid filler words. A sip of water is a simple, natural way to create a pause without breaking flow.

- **Handle technical hiccups gracefully:** If something goes wrong, maybe slides freeze or a demo fails, acknowledge it, move on, and return to the key message. Audiences are forgiving when they see a speaker adapt calmly. Having backup visuals or a recorded demo ensures you can recover quickly. By the time you arrive at the conference, you should know your material well enough to adapt if needed without losing the thread.

- **Be approachable afterward:** Some of your most valuable interactions will happen after the talk. Make yourself available to chat in the hallway, at networking events, or online. These conversations often provide deeper feedback and can lead to future collaborations. Don't forget to follow up with people you met at the event. Send a quick message referencing your conversation and, if relevant, propose a next step such as a collaboration, guest blog post, or joint webinar. Conference connections often become long-term partners.

- **Plan for contingencies**: Things will go wrong and you need to be prepared. In the case of a presentation, do this:

- Have your slides online somewhere—in case your local copy dies.

- Have a memory stick with your data on it, in case you need to use a computer that is hard-wired into the audio/video (AV) system.

- Prepare to not have your slides available and still be able to do a Q&A session.

- Don't expect any technology to be available—bring your own connectors, power cables, network cables...

- Don't expect to be able to go online—or turn on a hotspot on your mobile as backup if you really need to be.

- Aim for resolution independence and expect the worst possible color setting and low contrast. A good idea is to always leave plenty of border around your slides as many projectors cut content off.

- **Always reflect:** You're all done with your talk and every-thing went great! Or it went terrible and no one likes you, either way take some time to reflect on what went well and what went wrong and note it down so you can improve on it. Was there a particular section where people seemed like they were a little tuned out? Those are good signs that you may want to improve that section of the talk. Either go slower if it's a little too complicated, or make it more interesting if it's a little too boring, or drop the entire section if it's just not that interesting. What are people asking you about? That's a huge sign that they're either really interested in that portion of your talk or they're really confused about it still. It could also mean you did a poor

job at arguing that aspect and they still don't quite believe
you, which means that's a great place to start reworking
and improving to clarify your point better. After your talk,
you could also personally approach some attendees and
ask for constructive feedback. You want to stay constantly
improving your craft. speaking.io is a great comprehensive
resource for further speaking tips.

5.2.3 Event Sponsorships

Events are one of the few chances to build in-person trust at scale. They
create an environment where developers are open to discovering new
tools, meeting the people behind them, and asking questions they may not
bring to an online forum. Sponsorships amplify that opportunity by giving
you a formal presence.

But sponsorships are a high-cost, high-commitment play. Without
careful planning, they can drain budget and bandwidth for little return.

Even if you are not the DevRel leader or directly responsible for
deciding which events to sponsor, these insights will still serve you. Many
companies have a set list of recurring events they support each year.
The guidance in this section will help you contribute informed opinions
when those decisions are discussed and equip you to question whether a
sponsorship still delivers value.

How to Do Event Sponsorships Well

Choose Events That Will Serve You

Developer events are abundant, but only a fraction are worth sponsoring.
Your goal is to identify the ones that align with your objectives and deliver
a return on your investment.

- **Verify credibility**. Before committing to any sponsorship, assess the credibility and reputation of the event. The golden rule is never to sponsor an event you or a trusted peer have not attended before. You want firsthand insight into how well it is run, whether the schedule is reliable, whether the sessions attract high-quality and diverse speakers, and whether attendees match your target profile. If you cannot attend in advance, seek honest feedback from developers who have been there. Ask what they liked, what they did not, and whether the event is worth the investment.

- **Confirm audience fit**. A booth at a large, buzzy conference is worthless if it draws the wrong crowd for your product. Check attendee demographics, job titles, and the balance between decision-makers and hands-on implementers. Confirm that by attending, you will meet your target developers in meaningful numbers.

- **Avoid rigid packages**: Can you tailor your sponsorship so it represents your brand authentically? Can you secure a high-traffic or even reasonable-traffic location? If the package is rigid and uninspired, it may limit your ability to make an impact. Booth location is one of the most important factors in foot traffic. Work with event organizers early to review the floor plan and secure a high-traffic spot. Aim for areas near entrances, main walkways, or food and coffee stations. Avoid dead ends, back corners, or spots next to loud activities that make conversation difficult. If you cannot get a prime location, reconsider whether sponsorship is worth it.

Also, a cookie-cutter booth and a logo on a flyer are not enough. Look for chances to run demos, give talks, host workshops, or create experiences that reflect your product's strengths. Ask whether you can bring your own booth design, control your layout, or run interactive challenges.

- **Assess your capacity to execute**. Do you have the right team members, enough prep time, and the logistical support to pull it off? A half-hearted showing can do more damage to your brand than skipping the event altogether. If you don't have the capacity, then pass.

- **Confirm that you can afford it**. Plan the budget and resources in detail. Include sponsorship fees, travel and accommodation, booth materials, merch, shipping, demo equipment, and a buffer for unexpected costs.

Get ready to Show Up Well

Sponsorship only pays off if you make the most of the time, space, and attention you have at the event.

- **Define your anchor message**. Before you design the booth, build the demo, or decide what content to bring, decide on one clear message that will act as the backbone of your presence. Your product might have many features, but you only have seconds—maybe minutes—to connect with someone on the floor. Spreading yourself too thin dilutes your impact. Instead, pick one central message that connects the event audience's priorities to your product's strongest differentiator.

For example, if you are at a cloud infrastructure event and your product handles several things—monitoring, scaling, cost optimization, but you know attendees are currently obsessed with controlling cloud spend, your anchor message might be *"Cut your cloud bill by 40% without changing your architecture."* At Smallstep, we like to use "Achieve zero trust issues" or "You don't have to deal with threats from phishing anymore." Everything else at your booth: the demo, the merch, the content, the conversations, should then tie back to that anchor message.

- **Create a detailed event plan document**: Document everything in one place so your team knows exactly what to expect. Include the event name and date, venue address, booth location, setup times, staff schedules, contact information for everyone on the team, and all travel and accommodation details. Treat it like a playbook your colleagues can follow without you needing to be there to answer questions. This will come in handy for retrospectives also.

- **Match your event team to your expected audience**. The people working your booth are the face of your company. Make sure they have the skills and knowledge to connect with the attendees you want to attract. Never send a non-technical salesperson to engage with a technical crowd. If the event focuses on a language or framework your DevRel team does not cover, consider bringing in engineers from other teams. Coordinate their participation with their managers and prepare them with talking points, demo practice, and knowledge of your key messages.

- **Run pre-event marketing**: Do not rely on foot traffic alone. Let your community and existing customers know you will be there. Post on your blog, email your list, and share on social channels. Partner with the event organizer to get included in their official promotions. If you have a speaking slot, highlight it. If you have an interactive challenge or giveaway, tease it ahead of time. Give people a reason to find you on the floor.

- **Prepare a demo worth stopping for**: Your demo is part of your lead capture efforts, which we will discuss in more depth in point number 4. It should feel like magic in under a minute. That might be a transaction across your API, a real-time transformation of data, or something that changes state in a visually satisfying way. It must be live, not a canned video. Whoever is running the demo should practice until they can deliver it smoothly even when interrupted mid-sentence. The goal is to give people you engage with at your booth an "aha" moment that sticks in their mind and makes them want to learn more. And as expected, this demo should show how your product delivers on the promise made by your anchor message.

- **Prepare relevant content**: In addition to your demo, have materials that developers can access quickly for more information. You will not be able to answer every question or keep people at your booth for long conversations. Well-designed content can carry your product's presence into their workspace long after the event. This could be laminated cheat sheets, small fold-out guides, or QR codes linking to interactive examples or GitHub repos. Developers rarely keep materials they do not find genuinely useful, so avoid generic product brochures. Instead, create one-page explainers that show how your product solves a concrete pain point, command cheat sheets, feature comparison charts, or deep-dive resources like architecture diagrams, reference sheets, or sample configurations. Always tie everything back to your anchor message. If your sponsorship message is about reducing deployment time by 80%, every handout should reinforce that point—whether through case studies, workflow diagrams, or quick-start steps that show exactly how quickly someone can go live.

Upgrade Your Merch Game

Many teams default to stickers because they are cheap, light, and easy to distribute. The problem is that stickers rarely create lasting value. They usually end up in a swag bag, sometimes on a laptop if the design is exceptional, and are quickly forgotten. They do little to make you memorable after the event.

Instead, aim for merch that is different, practical, portable, and functional. Choose items useful enough to stay in someone's bag or on their desk for years, not days. Travel adapters, multi-port chargers, wallets, cable organizers, or quality backpacks all fit the bill. The goal is to make your brand part of the attendee's daily workflow or just something they would actually use; could be locally sourced bath bombs, coloring books for attendees' kids, or even umbrellas.

Get creative. Nobody needs another power bank or pen, notebook, water bottle, USB stick, T-shirt, or shitty sunglasses.

This approach may mean you hand out fewer items, but that is a strength, not a weakness. The people who receive them will be more aligned to your target audience, and you will have stronger opportunities for meaningful engagement. The trick is not to hand them out indiscriminately. Tie them to an action that integrates with your lead capture flow. This could be a short quiz, a puzzle, or a live coding challenge.

Done well, this approach delivers two benefits:

- It qualifies the person receiving the item, making it more likely they will remember your product because they interacted with it in a hands-on way.

- It gives your team a natural conversation hook, rather than simply handing something over and hoping it is remembered.

Design these challenges so they naturally attract the right audience. A DevOps company might offer a "deployment speed" puzzle where participants spot configuration errors in under two minutes. A data platform might run a quick data-cleaning challenge with a live leaderboard. Attendees outside your industry will usually self-select out, leaving you with higher-quality leads.

A few rules make this work better:

- Keep the action quick and painless. No one will complete a 15-field form for a water bottle.

- Make the merch visible but not piled up for anyone to grab without interaction.

- Train your booth staff to use the giveaway as part of the conversation, not as bait.

You can also add a third tier of high-value prizes such as an iPhone, a mechanical keyboard, cloud credits, or gift vouchers. Invite those who have completed the challenge and collected tier 2 merch to enter a raffle for a chance to win. This keeps them engaged longer and creates a natural reason to return to your booth later in the event.

Design Your Booth Flow for Lead Capture

Event sponsorships are not cheap. Your executives are definitely expecting some ROI from that budget. The main reason you sponsor events is to connect with the right people and turn those connections into future opportunities. How you design and position your booth will play a huge role in determining whether people walk past without a glance or stop to see what you have to offer.

If you're lucky, you snagged a good booth location, now it's time to make the most out of it. Many teams treat booth lead capture as "scan a badge, get an email." That's how you end up with a bloated, low-quality list that your sales team does not know what to do with. The goal is not to walk away with a bucket of contacts. It's to walk away with a curated set of high-value leads, each with context that lets you follow up in a personal, relevant way.

Think of your booth as a mini-experience with a beginning, middle, and end. The journey should naturally collect information without making the attendee feel interrogated.

Plan your space so the hook is at the edge (to stop people), conversation happens in a spot where you can hear each other, Demo station is visible and easy to step into, Lead capture is embedded into the conversation (staff enters notes while demoing or just after).

For example, you're sponsoring DevSecCon, a security-focused developer conference. Your product is an AI-powered static analysis tool that flags bugs, vulnerabilities, and security loopholes in code before commits are pushed. Your booth is 3m x 3m.

The Hook (Entry Point)

This is where you want to place something visual or interactive at the edge of your booth that stops people in their tracks.

First, you want to have your anchor message large, visible at the top: "Accept pull requests without regrets. Find and fix security issues in seconds, not hours."

Then, at the outer edge of your booth, you want to set up a large vertical monitor displaying a live "Find the Vulnerability" challenge. Attendees see a snippet of code on screen with a big headline:

"Think you can spot the bug faster than our AI? Spot the error and win."

Every 2 minutes, the snippet changes—some show obvious errors, others have subtle security flaws. A small timer counts down, adding urgency. Beneath the monitor, keep a small stack of visible, practical merch (wallets, travel adapters, mechanical keyboards) to signal that prizes are real.

When an attendee sees the challenge and walks up, a staffer says: "Want to try our 2-minute code challenge? Spot the security loophole and win a prize." After their effort, the staffer hands them a merch item, and then strikes up a conversation to move them along to the next stage of the lead capture. Something like: "So that took you about one minute to spot, that's one minute you could be drinking coffee. Can I show you how fast it would have taken our tool to find that?" That then moves them into the conversation zone.

The Conversation and Lead Capture (Middle Point)

The conversation zone should be clearly separated from the hook zone. This could be as simple as a small partition or a layout that guides people naturally from one area to the other. Once a developer engages with your hook and decides to see a demo, they should transition smoothly from the hook person to the demo presenter.

Assign specific roles—greeter, demo presenter, lead capturer—so nothing is missed. Rotate roles to keep energy high. Even with strong tools and a clear plan, poor execution can ruin lead quality. Everyone working the booth should be trained to

- Start and end conversations naturally

- Move from small talk to lead capture without making it feel forced.

- Log notes discreetly so the interaction still feels human and personal.

Role-play the entire journey from hook to exit until it feels seamless. Create a cheat sheet of qualifying questions and practice capturing context in under 30 seconds after each conversation.

Your demo should take no more than two minutes and tie directly to your anchor message. If your anchor message is *"Accept pull requests without regrets. Find and fix security issues in seconds, not hours,"* show it happening in real time.

For example, start a pull request, let your AI tool instantly flag errors, explain why they're problematic, suggest a fix, and explain why the fix is better.

From there, the demo presenter should ask qualifying and context questions such as

- "What do you think?"

- "What's your review process like at your company?"

- "What's the biggest pain point you have with that?"

- "Do you run security scans before or after you commit?"

- "What's the trickiest bug you've caught before it hit production?"

These are not filler questions. They are designed to uncover high-quality leads. Strong signals include

- They work in security-conscious industries (finance, healthcare, regulated SaaS).

- They use competitors like Snyk or SonarQube.

- They have manual code review bottlenecks.

While the conversation is happening, the lead capturer should record key context in your CRM or lead form—not just the contact's name and email, but

- Current tool or solution they use

- Pain point mentioned

- Features or benefits they reacted to most

- Their role

- Feedback given

- Personal details that make follow-up more human ("Migrating to AWS next quarter")

- Follow-up asset promised (guide, trial, pricing sheet, webinar link)

When the demo ends, hand the lead off to the exit point.

The Exit (Last Point)

The exit point is your opportunity to leave a lasting impression and set up the next touchpoint. This is your moment to turn a good interaction into an ongoing conversation.

Before the attendee leaves, offer them something that feels like a direct continuation of the discussion they just had, not a generic sales handoff. Use this moment to hand out any physical or digital content that reinforces your anchor message. For example, if your sponsorship message is about finding security issues "in seconds, not hours," give them a quick-start guide, case study, or workflow diagram that proves the point.

Top it off by having a challenge or raffle that challenges attempts and participants can enter into. Let them know how to check the leaderboard, when winners will be announced, and what the grand prize is. For multi-day events, this creates a reason for them to return to your booth, whether it is to see if they have won, improve their score, or collect a prize.

The key is to make the exit feel like the natural next step in your conversation, something they want, that ties directly to their needs, and that opens the door for follow-up after the event.

Follow Up, Measure, and Refine

Sponsorships only deliver long-term value if you turn event interactions into ongoing conversations and use what you learned to improve for next time.

- **Prioritize timely follow-up**: Follow-up should begin while the memory of the interaction is still fresh. Contact leads within 48 hours, ideally the same day, and reference the exact conversation or demo they experienced so your outreach feels personal rather than generic. Something like, "Hello X, we met last week at DevSecCon and you mentioned that you wanted to see a demo of yzw ..." Because you captured this contextual information during the lead capture phase, you're positioned to do this.

- **Run a structured retrospective within one week of the event**: Involve everyone who participated: DevRel, marketing, sales, product, and engineering if they contributed. Review what went well, such as traffic flow, demo engagement, or merch appeal; what could be

improved, such as booth layout, qualifying process, or
messaging clarity; and what to try next time, whether that is
a new hook, a different merch challenge, or better prep
materials. Keep the discussion candid and focused on
learning rather than justifying sunk costs.

- **Measure and report ROI in the context of your goals**:
Capture and share the full story of the event. Record lead
counts, the number of hot leads, meetings booked, demos
delivered, and content distributed. Include qualitative
notes from the booth team about what worked and where
they struggled. Go beyond counting badge scans and track
how many leads converted into trials, opportunities, or
customers. Consider secondary metrics such as new
partnerships, press coverage, or community engagement. If
the event was more about brand presence than direct sales,
measure against brand-specific criteria set in advance,
such as social mentions, newsletter sign-ups, or the reach
of a speaking slot. Senior leadership responds well to clear,
evidence-backed results, and reports like this make it easier
to secure budgets for future events.

- **Build and maintain an event history**: Keep a central
record of event reports so you can identify patterns over
time. This will show which events produce the most value,
which sponsorship tiers are worth the investment, and
which formats—such as speaking, booths, or workshops—
perform best. This history becomes an essential reference
when deciding whether to renew a sponsorship or
experiment with a new event.

Figure 5-2 summarises the event sponsorship lifecycle as a
continuous cycle.

Figure 5-2. *The Event Sponsorship Lifecycle*

5.2.4 Blog Posts

Some of the most enduring developer content lives on blogs. They are
searchable, shareable, and skimmable. When done well, blog posts can
drive long-tail traffic for years, surface in AI assistants, and appear in
Slack threads or internal wikis just when someone needs them. They are
a versatile format that can support nearly every stage of the developer
journey, from discovery to decision to deep implementation.

But "write a blog post" is a vague instruction. About what? In what
style? To what end?

Here's an unpopular take: you should no longer be writing top-of-
funnel definition content like *"What is serverless computing?"* or *"How a
REST API works."* These types of posts have lost their value. Developers
now turn to AI tools for those answers, and those tools are faster and often
more accurate. Generic explainers no longer pull their weight. They rarely
drive activation or adoption.

This shift is not a loss. In fact, it's an opportunity.

For years, SEO strategies forced teams to churn out generic content to satisfy search algorithms. Many of those posts had little to do with the product itself. But traffic that doesn't lead to action, understanding, or trust is vanity. It creates noise, not value. We'll return to this idea when we discuss metrics. For now, think of the decline of SEO-driven content as a welcome constraint. It forces us to create content that developers actually want and need.

Here's a simple rule of thumb:

If AI can generate it accurately, it's probably not worth writing.

How to Do Blog Posts Well

So what is worth writing?

The answer is content that helps developers solve real problems, understand trade-offs, and see how your product fits into their world. Blog posts should serve both your audience and your product's goals. They should be useful, trustworthy, and grounded in experience.

When you write, you want to be able to connect that to value in some way to your company. The ultimate goal is to encourage readers to try out the product (or at least recognize that your product exists in case they're ever in the market). It's achieved not by flashy advertisements, but rather by embedding the product into a genuinely intriguing and educational post is a highly effective way of getting the attention of programmers.

Find Ideas That Matter

Look for moments where your product overlaps with a real developer's need, and where your experience can help close that gap. One company that I really like and which does this well is Fly.io.

- **What problems are new users consistently having?**

  If support tickets or Discord questions keep surfacing the same confusion, write the post that clears it up. Example: "How to Set Up Email Sending with Our API in Under 10 Minutes."

- **What trade-offs does your product help navigate?**

  Use blog posts to explain *how* your product works and *why* certain decisions were made. Example: "Why Our Database Client Uses Persistent Connections by Default."

- **What took longer to figure out than expected?**

  If you had to cobble together five GitHub issues and two half-baked blog posts to get something working, write the canonical version.

- **What do you keep repeating in demos, calls, or internal Slack threads?**

  If you've explained the same thing three times in three different formats, it's a good blog candidate. Or maybe there's a specific bug that customer engineering has had to help users who code in a specific environment fix a couple of times?

- **What internal engineering work made your product stronger?**

  Case studies, rewrites, bug hunts, and lessons learned help build trust in your team's technical competence and also builds trust in your product. Example: "How We Shaved 300ms Off Our API Response Times by Rewriting Our Rate Limiter in Rust"

- **What makes your product opinionated, and why?**

  If you made an unconventional choice, talk about it.
  Developers respect strong, well-defended opinions.
  Example: "Why We Don't Support Webhooks (and
  What We Recommend Instead)."

Check That Your Idea Is Worth Reading

Writing a blog post is not the goal. Creating something that is read, remembered, and shared is. A compelling topic earns the initial click, but a thoughtful, well-executed post is what sustains attention and builds trust. Use the checklist below to test whether your idea is worth developing:

- **Is it specific?** Broad posts feel vague. Specific posts feel useful. Specificity earns clicks and respect.

  - **Better**: "How We Reduced CI Time by 40% Using
    Parallel Jobs in GitHub Actions"

  - **Weaker**: "Optimizing Your CI Pipeline"

- **Is it grounded in experience?** The best posts reflect real decisions, real pain, or real improvements. Developers trust firsthand accounts over vague suggestions. Details give your post credibility, and make it harder to forget.

  - **Better**: "What We Learned Rewriting Our Auth Flow in
    NextAuth After Burning Two Weeks on OAuth Bugs"

  - **Weaker**: "Best Practices for Authentication in
    Modern Apps"

- **Does it say something new or differently?** You don't have to invent a new concept. But you should bring a fresh angle, metaphor, or voice. Posts that repackage existing ideas in a clear, memorable way are just as valuable as novel insights. Surprise or delight your reader—even slightly—and they'll stick with you.

  - **Better**: "Explaining Rate Limiting Using Airport Security Lines"

  - **Weaker**: "What Is Rate Limiting?"

- **Does it align with product value without sounding like a sales pitch?** Great developer content builds trust and interest. It doesn't need to beg for a signup. Frame your product as the answer to a real, shared problem.

  - **Better**: "A Reliable Way to Rotate Secrets Without Restarting Your App

  - **Weaker**: "Why You Should Use Our Secret Manager Today"

- **Would you bookmark it, share it, or send it to a teammate?** If the answer is no, then neither will your audience. Ask yourself: would I share this post during a real engineering incident or onboarding session? If not, why not?

  - **Better**: "How to Debug Mutual TLS Failures in Production Using OpenSSL"

  - **Weaker**: "TLS Explained"

Use Templates for Guidance and Ease

Once you've landed on a strong idea, the next challenge is figuring out how to bring it to life. What's the best angle? What shape should the story take? Where do you even begin?

Templates help you answer these questions. They give you structure when the blank page feels overwhelming and help you get to a solid first draft faster.

Most of the blog post ideas you'll come up with will fall into one of these broad categories:

- **Tutorials and How-Tos**: Teaching someone how to build, integrate, or use something

- **Case Studies and Retrospectives**: Sharing what your team built and why, including trade-offs and behind-the-scenes decisions

- **Thought Leadership and Opinions**: Offering a perspective on a technical trend or topic to shape how developers think

- **Benchmarks and Comparisons**: Helping developers evaluate tools or approaches using real data and performance metrics

- **Product Perspectives and Announcements**: Explaining not just what your team released but why you built it and how it solves a real problem

For each of these categories, there are tested and trusted templates that can help you start writing sooner, organize your thoughts clearly, and reduce the friction of getting stuck. They're not rigid formulas. Think of them as scaffolding: they help you build a strong draft while still leaving space for your voice, your team's story, and your reader's context.

A good template also makes collaboration easier. It gives you something concrete to share with engineers, subject matter experts, or other stakeholders when co-writing a post. It helps clarify expectations, spark ideas, and even speed up the feedback process.

Piotr Sarna and Cynthia Dunlop covered a couple of templates in their book, *Writing for Developers* (blogs that get read), that really helped me:

Template 1: How We/I Built It

This template is ideal when you're sharing something your team built, improved, or refactored. It could be a new feature, a platform rewrite, or an internal tool that made the product better. It works well for case studies and product perspectives, especially when your goal is to show how your team thinks through problems, makes technical decisions, and builds systems that last.

It can also be used to tell the story of how you solved a real-world problem using your own product. Sometimes the story comes from an individual developer building something valuable with your tool. Other times, it is a customer or partner who used your platform, API, or library to unlock a meaningful outcome. In all these cases, the act of building is the narrative lens. What was created matters, but the focus is on how and why it came to life.

The goal is not simply to present the outcome. It is to make readers feel like they were there in the room, a part of the process. You want them to see the decisions made, the bugs encountered, the paths that failed, and the lessons learned. A well-written post of this kind builds technical trust and gives your team a human face.

Make sure to include what went wrong and how you adapted. These moments help readers relate to your process and build credibility. Use visuals to make your points clearer. Diagrams, before-and-after metrics, and code snippets can all help ground the post. Let the team's personality come through in the voice and tone. Avoid flattening the story by skipping straight to the solution, or making vague claims like "we improved performance" without showing the evidence.

Suggested structure

1. **Start with the trigger:** What problem or opportunity made this work necessary? What was breaking down or holding people back?

2. **Set the context:** Give readers the landscape: what constraints, priorities, or goals shaped your decisions.

3. **Walk through the process:** Take us step-by-step through the evolution. Highlight where you tried things that didn't work, and why you shifted course.

4. **Explain the outcome:** What's better now? What changed in the product, experience or performance? Did it reduce latency? Improve reliability? Save developer hours? Clarify the outcome and who it benefited.

5. **Reflect on what you learned:** What insights emerged along the way? What advice would you give another team attempting something similar? Share what surprised you, what you'd do differently, or what other teams might borrow from your experience.

6. **Tie it back to product value:** This part is subtle but important. How does this reinforce the value of your product or approach? What impression should the reader walk away with about what your company prioritizes or enables?

Example:

"You Can Have Zero Downtime Certificate Rotation Without Restarting Apps"

- **Problem**: Many production systems rely on certificates for mTLS or service-to-service auth. Rotating those certificates often requires restarting applications—which introduces risk, causes downtime, or adds friction for dev teams.

- **Constraints**: Customers wanted seamless rotation, but our infrastructure relied on long-lived processes. We needed to rework our reload logic while preserving compatibility with existing setups.

- **Approach**: We explored several reload strategies—signals, sockets, sidecars. Eventually, we settled on watching the certificate file for changes and using Go's GetCertificate callback to dynamically serve new ones. We also updated our CLI to support short-lived certs and safe overwrite patterns.

- **Results**: With this system, customers can rotate certificates every 12 hours or even more frequently without touching running services. It improves security posture without hurting uptime.

- **Takeaway**: The reader walks away not just understanding how you built something smart but also trusting your team's technical chops and your product's reliability. They also now see your product as one that handles edge cases and operational pain with elegance, which influences their perception when evaluating your category.

Alternate scenario:

"How I Built a Free Personal VPN in 15 Minutes"

This variation uses the same structure, but from an individual developer's point of view. It is especially useful when telling a story about how someone used your product to solve a real-world problem. Whether it is written by someone on your team or an external contributor, the post reads like a first-person narrative and doubles as both a testimonial and a tutorial.

Template 2: Bug Hunt

This template is ideal for documenting a tricky issue that was difficult to identify, reproduce, or resolve. The bug might have been discovered internally by your team or surfaced through user feedback, support tickets, or community reports. In both cases, you're telling the story of how your team handles friction points and makes the product better over time.

Bug hunt posts work best when they mirror the kinds of investigations other developers might have to run themselves. By walking readers through the signals, false leads, and eventual fix, you give them a valuable reference—and build credibility by showing how your team works under uncertainty. These posts can also serve as real-time documentation of your engineering values: curiosity, rigor, and responsiveness to user needs.

They're often highly technical and tend to rank well over time if the issue is common or the fix is unintuitive. In fact, many developers find these posts through search. That's why it helps when the title includes the exact error message or symptom.

You don't need a high-severity outage to use this format. Some of the best posts come from smaller bugs that took days to debug. If it's the kind of issue others are likely to run into—or one that exposed a surprising system behavior—it's worth writing about.

Suggested structure:

- **Start with the symptom:** What did users or engineers observe? Include any logs, error messages, or behavior that signaled the issue.

- **Explain the context:** What triggered the problem? Was it a recent change, an environment-specific bug, or something that emerged under scale?

- **Walk through the investigation:** How did you try to reproduce the issue? What signals or logs guided your process? Don't skip the dead ends—they humanize the story and make it more trustworthy.

- **Show the root cause:** What exactly was going wrong, and why? Be as specific and detailed as needed for a technical reader to follow along.

- **Explain the fix:** How did you solve the issue? Did you patch code, change configuration, update documentation, or rethink an architectural assumption?

- **Close with the takeaway:** What can other teams learn from this incident? How can they avoid similar issues, and what should they keep in mind going forward?

Example

"If Your Auth Requests Are Hanging in Production (This Is Probably Why)"

- **Scene:** We started receiving sporadic reports of login attempts timing out, but only in specific regions and mostly during traffic spikes.

- **Symptom:** Service logs showed timeouts when connecting to our external identity provider. But the provider's metrics looked healthy, and we couldn't reproduce the issue in staging.

- **Investigation:** We added distributed tracing and deeper logs, ran synthetic tests across multiple network paths, and even suspected DNS resolution at one point. None of those theories held up.

- **Root Cause:** After several days of investigation, we discovered that a recent code change had accidentally removed a timeout configuration in our HTTP client. As a result, under certain traffic conditions, requests would hang indefinitely rather than timing out and retrying as designed.

- **Fix:** We added an explicit timeout, deployed a patch, and confirmed the issue was resolved across all regions. We also added tests to ensure default timeouts are present in future releases.

- **Impact:** The fix restored reliability to our login flow and reduced authentication latency by 15%.

- **Takeaway:** Even small configuration changes can lead to serious consequences. This incident reinforced the importance of treating timeouts and retries as first-class concerns during code reviews.

Template 3: Thoughts on Trend

This template is a great fit when your team wants to take a clear, informed stance on a topic that's currently shaping developer conversations. It could be a popular belief that deserves pushback, an emerging tool or practice you think is being misapplied, or a shift in the ecosystem that needs better framing. These kinds of posts help your company stand out by offering clarity where others are adding noise.

This isn't about hot takes. It's about helping developers make better choices, using your team's technical experience and point of view to reframe how they evaluate the space you operate in.

The strongest ones are built on lived experience. Maybe you've seen a widely recommended best practice backfire in your environment. Maybe you've watched teams struggle because they adopted a shiny tool that didn't scale with their needs. You're not writing to be provocative or to pitch your product. You're writing to build trust. Trust that your team understands the trade-offs. Trust that your product is shaped by people who've wrestled with these decisions. And trust that your company is a thoughtful voice in the space, not just a vendor with a loud microphone.

Suggested structure:

- **Start with the tension:** What common assumption or growing trend is your team challenging, questioning, or trying to reframe? Make it tangible. Use a real scenario or belief that your readers would recognize.

- **Make the case:** Explain why this trend deserves scrutiny. What is being overlooked? What trade-offs are being ignored? Use clear arguments, technical examples, data, or user patterns to build credibility.

- **Offer a better lens:** Help the reader shift how they think about the topic. What should they be considering instead? What principles or mental models does your team use that might help them?

- **Tie into your product's philosophy:** You don't have to pitch directly, but give a glimpse into how your product or approach is better suited for the new reality. This helps readers understand what your company values— and why that matters.

- **Close with a strong takeaway:** End with a clear insight that's easy to remember, share, or act on. You want the reader to walk away feeling smarter and more confident in how they think about the issue.

Example: "3 Reasons Why You Shouldn't Use Public CAs for Internal Infrastructures"

I wrote this piece while I worked at Smallstep and it is a perfect example of a Thoughts on X piece. This post went on to the top of Hacker News and became quite popular.

- **Tension:** Everyone uses Let's Encrypt and other public Certificate Authorities (CAs) because they're free and easy. But internal infrastructure needs are different.

- **Argument:** Public CAs are rate-limited, inflexible, expose metadata in CT logs, and can't issue certs for private domains. These limitations create friction and security risks for internal teams.

- **Perspective shift:** Internal systems deserve the same rigor as production websites—but with different constraints and requirements. A private CA gives you the flexibility, control, and safety you need.

- **Product connection:** The post doesn't pitch early. Instead, it ends by showing that Smallstep makes it easy to run a private CA without the overhead.

- **Takeaway:** Public CAs are great for the public web.
  But for internal systems, they're often a bad fit, and the
  risks are real. It's better to use a CA built specifically for
  internal tooling like Smallstep's step-CA.

Template 4: Lessons Learned

This template is best used when your team has gone through a meaningful
experience—whether a launch, an outage, a project pivot, direction
change, encountered unexpected edge cases in production, or even a
failed initiative—and come out the other side with new clarity. The goal
is to reflect on that experience with honesty and depth, and share the hard-
won takeaways that other developers or teams can learn from. It is ideal for
both **case studies** and **thought leadership** categories.

A Lessons Learned post isn't just a retrospective. It's a chance to
demonstrate how your team thinks and improves. It shows maturity,
builds credibility, and gives others a chance to learn from your mistakes
and insights. It's also a subtle way to highlight how your product's vision
and development are grounded in real-world learning, not ivory tower
idealism.

Lessons Learned posts work best when you avoid sugarcoating.
You don't need to manufacture drama, but be honest about what was
confusing, risky, or uncomfortable. Readers resonate more with "here's
what we got wrong" than with polished success stories that read like PR.

Suggested structure:

- **Set the scene:** What was the initiative or event? Why
  did it matter? Briefly explain what your team attempted
  or went through.

- **Name the turning point:** What didn't go as expected?
  What was the moment that made you pause, rethink, or
  shift course?

- **Walk through the key learnings:** These might be technical insights, process changes, team coordination lessons, or user behavior surprises. Be specific, and where possible, show the before-and-after.

- **Connect it to your product or approach:** What did this experience change about how your team builds, designs, or supports your product? What's different going forward?

- **Offer advice or principles:** End with a few takeaways that another team could apply in a similar situation. Make the post valuable beyond your internal context.

Example: "We Tried Moving Our SDK Docs to Notion. Here's Why We Moved Back."

This should not be about shaming a tool like Notion. It's about showing the decision-making process, the trade-offs, where things went sideways, and what was taken away. The tone should be generous.

- **Scene**: A devtool startup moved its SDK documentation to Notion, hoping to speed up editing, lower the barrier for contributions, and let marketing help out.

- **Friction**: Within weeks, support tickets increased. Developers couldn't find endpoints easily, code formatting broke on mobile, and SEO traffic tanked.

- **Learnings**: What worked for internal wikis didn't work for documentation meant to be embedded into developer workflows. Notion lacked proper search semantics, API versioning support, and Git-based review.

- **Product impact**: They migrated back to a static doc site using Docusaurus, added Algolia search, and invested in a clear contribution guide instead. They also built a Markdown preview tool so non-devs could collaborate without breaking syntax.

- **Advice to others**: Don't confuse internal ease of editing with user experience. If your docs are a core part of your product, treat them with the same discipline. Developers need speed, structure, and search—not just access.

Template 5: Benchmarks and Test Results

This template is ideal for showcasing performance data or real-world tests, especially when engineers are the audience. These readers are hungry for hard numbers, side-by-side comparisons, and meaningful insights that help them make informed decisions. But they also come skeptical. Benchmark posts are presumed guilty of bias until proven innocent, so your job is to build trust through precision, transparency, and clarity.

The best of these posts are rigorous, reproducible, and unapologetically nerdy. They're formal in tone, more like technical studies than blogs. The data takes center stage, and the visuals must tell a clear story, not just look pretty. That means charts and tables that highlight differences at a glance, label what's better, and avoid misleading visual cues. A post like this should also be accompanied by full documentation: what was tested, why, how, and with what constraints. If the benchmark can't be reproduced or justified, readers will dismiss it, and likely your product too.

Done well, benchmark blog posts can serve as both technical education and a valuable sales collateral. These can be posts for

- Tests that compare the company's product against its competition

- Tests that compare something (such as cloud infrastructure or hardware) using the company's product

- Measuring something independent of the company's products (e.g., an open source project or a new graphics processing unit)

.**Suggested Structure**

- **Start with the test goal:** What were you trying to measure or compare? What practical question were you answering for yourself or your audience?

- **Explain the setup:** Describe the test environment in detail: hardware specs, cloud configurations, OS versions, software versions, and any special tuning. Justify your choices and call out constraints.

- **Present the results:** Use visuals that make the story obvious. Charts should show deltas, not just raw values. Stack comparisons side by side where possible. Label what's better—and why.

- **Interpret what it means:** Don't just show the numbers. Explain what they mean for different types of users or scenarios. Call out trade-offs. Be honest about where your product doesn't win.

- **Share limitations and next steps:** If you didn't get to test something, say so. If there are other configurations or workloads worth exploring, mention them. If you plan to re-run the tests later, let readers know.

- **Link to how to reproduce it:** If the reader can't recreate your test, they won't trust it. Link to the full code, configs, or steps used. Bonus points if it's in a public repo.

- **Invite conversation, not controversy:** If you're comparing with competitors, write with a tone of clarity and humility. You're here to inform, not dunk. Let the data speak, and be ready to update the post if feedback surfaces valid issues.

Example: **"Redpanda vs. Kafka: A performance benchmark"**
Redpanda's blog post "Redpanda vs. Kafka: A performance benchmark" is a great example. It compares Redpanda to Kafka on real-world workloads and cloud configurations, using open-source tooling and test setups the reader can reproduce.

- **Context:** Redpanda set out to compare its performance against Apache Kafka using a set of realistic workloads and cloud-based configurations.

- **Setup:** The team used open-source benchmarking tools and cloud environments to simulate real-world conditions. They included detailed specs for hardware, software versions, and configuration settings to ensure reproducibility.

- **Results:** The benchmark included side-by-side comparisons showing throughput and latency across various workloads. Charts were clearly labeled, with better performance visually highlighted.

- **Interpretation:** The authors walked through each result, explaining where Redpanda outperformed Kafka and why. They also noted test limitations, including areas where they would have liked to run more balanced comparisons.

- **Takeaway:** The post is confident but measured. It presents Redpanda as a technically superior alternative while acknowledging trade-offs and avoiding hype. The inclusion of methodology, source tools, and reproducibility details builds reader trust and reinforces the credibility of the data.

Finish Strong

A strong idea and good structure are not enough. To make your blog post publishable and worth sharing, you need to finish well. That means tightening your draft, seeking useful feedback, managing your metadata, and polishing the piece so it performs across different channels.

Don't treat editing as cleanup. It is where a decent post becomes one people bookmark, share, or learn from.

Here is how to do it:

Tighten the Draft

Cut anything that doesn't serve the reader. Remove throat-clearing intros. Eliminate softeners like "a bit," "somewhat," and "can be helpful." Trim repetitive phrasing. If you find yourself saying something twice in two ways, pick one. Use concrete, specific language. Every sentence should move the piece forward.

Check the Shape and Scannability

Look at your headings and subheadings. Do they guide the reader through the piece clearly? Are your visuals doing real work, or just filling space? If a screenshot needs a caption, write one. If a code block isn't immediately clear, add a sentence that explains what it does and why it matters. Use bold text sparingly to avoid visual clutter. Skimmability builds trust and keeps readers engaged.

Get the Right Kind of Feedback

Before publishing, share your draft with someone who can reflect your target audience. This might be a teammate, an engineer outside your immediate group, a product manager, a developer advocate, or someone in support who has context on the problem. Don't ask, "What do you think?" Ask specific questions like: "Is the setup too long?" "Is this where you'd stop reading?" "Does this part feel clear or confusing?" "Would you share this in our team Slack?" Early feedback improves quality and reduces the need for rewrites later.

Write the Title and Description Last

A good title is clear, specific, and compelling. Try a few versions. If it sounds like AI wrote it, try again. A strong title makes a promise and delivers on it. The description should summarize what the post offers in one short sentence. This shows up in search engines, social cards, and internal link previews, so clarity matters.

Check Metadata and Assets

Add relevant tags for sorting and search. Set the author name if your system doesn't do it automatically. Double-check the publish date and make sure the post has a proper preview image. The image should be readable and recognizable when shrunk down to thumbnail size. If your blog shows reading time or contributor bios, make sure those are correct too.

Optimize for Multi-platform Use

Assume the post will show up in Slack threads, search engine results, social media previews, and possibly even AI tools. Make sure the intro explains the value quickly. A reader should be able to tell what the post is about and why it's useful within the first few sentences. Avoid overusing internal references or inside jokes that won't make sense outside your team.

Do a Final Reader Pass

Before you publish, skim your post like someone who is busy and looking
for answers. Does the piece hook attention quickly? Are key points easy to
find? Does the flow feel natural? Fix anything that creates friction.

5.2.5 Documentation

Documentation is a broad, well-studied discipline, with entire books like
Docs for Developers and *Modern Technical Writing* devoted to teaching
teams how to build it from scratch. For this section, we will focus on
improving the documentation you already have, spotting opportunities to
make it work harder for your DevRel goals and adding new pieces where
they will have the most impact.

Sometimes your DevRel team will include a technical writer, and
documentation will fall under their care; other times, that responsibility
will belong to a Developer Experience Engineer or a Developer Advocate.

Documentation is a core part of the developer journey and, when done
well, one of the most effective levers DevRel can pull to influence adoption,
activation, and retention. Strong documentation accelerates the path from
curiosity to habit. Weak documentation slows adoption, increases support
load, and limits community self-help.

How to Do Documentation Well

"Good" documentation can be hard to define without a framework. This
is where two complementary tools come in. The Diátaxis framework
helps you structure documentation so each piece serves a clear purpose
in the developer journey. The Good Docs Project provides ready-to-use
templates so you can create high-quality pages faster, without starting from
a blank screen. Together, they make it easier to improve what you have, fill
gaps, and maintain a consistent standard over time.

Build a Clear Doc Structure with Diátaxis

One of the most developer-respected approaches to building and improving documentation is the **Diátaxis framework**. It offers a framework for recognizing discernible information patterns within documentation. The approach defines distinct information types or patterns just like for blog posts, which helps writers recognize structures for organizing content tailored to specific user goals.

Diátaxis is valuable for DevRel because it answers a key question: *How can we make our documentation serve developers better without burning months on a massive rewrite?* Its strength lies in encouraging small, iterative improvements rather than imposing a perfect structure up front. Like tending a garden, you prune, replant, and water the section you are standing in, letting the overall shape emerge as it grows. Documentation does not need to be "finished" to be useful; it only needs to be healthy, complete for its stage, and ready for the next step.

Diátaxis divides documentation into four categories based on the reader's need:

- **Tutorials:** For learning by doing, for new users looking to onboard quickly

- **How-to guides:** For achieving specific goals, for intermediate users solving specific problems

- **Reference:** For looking up precise information, for experts needing precise information

- **Explanation:** For understanding concepts, to provide deeper understanding

Let's briefly discuss each one.

Tutorials

In the Diátaxis framework, tutorials are learning-oriented. They teach by guiding
a developer through a meaningful, achievable goal. Along the way, the learner
acquires new concepts, skills, and familiarity with tools. The focus is not on
simply getting something done but on building capability and confidence.

The finished app, configuration, or project is not the real prize. The
real value lies in what the learner gains during the process. For example:
Build and deploy your first secure API with our platform. You'll set up an
environment, implement authentication, create endpoints, and deploy,
picking up multiple skills, even if the API will never be used in production.

Tutorials often feel longer and more hand-held than other doc types
because they walk with the learner through unfamiliar territory. They use
the "we" voice ("We'll set up the project together") to create a sense of
shared progress.

Think of it like teaching a child to cook. A lesson framed as *"Learn to
make a three-course Italian dinner"* is really about knife skills, cooking
techniques, and timing. The recipe—the finished dish—is just the
structure for the learning experience. The child gains skills by doing them
alongside you, not from explanations. Whether the dish turns out perfectly
is irrelevant; what matters is that they had a small success, enjoyed the
process, and want to return to the kitchen.

A successful tutorial works the same way. Its goal is not for the learner
to memorize every step but for them to leave with new skills, a sense of
accomplishment, and the confidence to keep building. The best tutorials
in DevRel send developers away with something working, a clearer sense
of how your product fits into their world, and motivation to keep going.

Tutorials are often confused with how-to guides, overloaded with
explanation, or packed with options that distract rather than teach. The
challenge is to design a path that delivers just enough information at the
right moment, produces visible results early, and builds a steady rhythm of
doing and seeing results.

- **Sets a clear destination from the start:** Let the learner know exactly where they are headed: "By the end of this tutorial, you will have built and deployed a scalable web application." Avoid promising what they will "learn," which can feel presumptuous; focus on what they will accomplish.

- **Delivers visible results early and often:** Learning comes from connecting cause to effect. Every step should produce something tangible, such as a terminal output, a visible UI change, or a passing test, to build trust that the end goal is within reach.

- **Keeps explanations short and the learner in action:** In a tutorial, the learner's focus is on following directions and getting results. Long explanations break that rhythm. Keep them brief ("We're using HTTPS for security—see this link for more") and link to reference or explanation docs for deeper reading.

- **Guides the learner down one reliable path:** Multiple options force the learner to stop, weigh choices, and wonder if they picked the "right" one. This adds cognitive load and increases the risk of going off-track. Save variations, optimizations, and alternative workflows for how-to guides or explanation pages.

- **Maintains a narrative of what to expect:** Reduce anxiety by telling the learner what should happen: "You will see a green check mark appear" or "The server should return a 200 OK response." Include likely error states and how to fix them.

- **Prompts reflection by pointing out what to notice:**
  Learners often focus so much on the next step that
  they miss important signs or patterns. Draw attention
  to these moments—how a prompt changes, why a log
  line appears, or what a visual change means—to turn
  repetition into deeper learning.

- **Uses "we" language to create shared progress:** Speak
  as if you and the learner are on the journey together:
  "First, we'll create the project directory. Then we'll
  install the dependencies." The first-person plural
  reduces distance, builds rapport, and reinforces that
  the learner is not alone. Pair this with unambiguous
  instructions and affirmations of progress to keep them
  oriented.

How-to Guides

How-to guides are for getting something done. They give step-by-step
instructions for achieving a specific outcome, assuming the reader already
has some background knowledge. The journey doesn't matter; only the
result does.

Where tutorials serve the acquisition of skill (learning something new),
how-to guides serve the application of skill (getting something done). They
assume the reader has at least some familiarity with the tools or domain.
The reader comes with a clear goal in mind, and your job is to give them
exactly the steps to achieve it. Nothing more, nothing less.

A tutorial is like a simulation: a safe, guided environment where you
can learn by building something "real enough," but where the main point
is practice and understanding, not production use.

- **Example (tutorial)**: Build a "To-do app" with Node JS. It teaches you concepts you can later apply to your own project, but the app itself isn't meant to run in production. But, by the end, you've learned multiple skills.

A how-to guide is like a production recipe: it gives you the exact, tested steps to achieve a specific outcome in the real world. You follow it when you have a working system and a clear goal to accomplish now.

- **Example (how-to)**: *Enable JWT authentication on an existing API.* This assumes you already know what an API is and have one running. It gives you the exact commands and configuration changes to enable JWT, nothing more. There's no teaching about what JWT is or why it's secure, just links to explanations, if needed.

Tying it further to our cooking analogy, a recipe is the perfect model for a how-to guide. It starts with a clear outcome ("How to bake a sourdough loaf"), gives you the exact ingredients and tools, and walks you through the process in logical order. It assumes you already know the basics—preheating the oven, measuring flour—and focuses entirely on the sequence needed to get the result. Just like a good recipe, a good how-to guide anticipates challenges, gives you the right step at the right moment, and leaves you with exactly what you set out to create.

A strong how-to guide typically has these characteristics:

- **Written for a reader who knows what they want:** The audience is not here to explore. They have a specific outcome in mind, and you can assume they know the basics and can follow instructions without extra handholding.

- **Focuses on action, not theory:** Every step should move the reader toward the goal. Keep them in execution mode by linking to deeper explanations instead of embedding them in the guide.

- **Addresses real-world complexity:** Real projects rarely match ideal examples. Offer room for judgment calls, exceptions, and adaptations, but keep the main path clear so the reader never loses sight of the goal.

- **Is logically ordered for efficiency and flow:** Arrange instructions so they feel natural and streamlined. Minimize unnecessary context-switching between tools or environments, and sequence tasks to set up later steps for success.

- **Is practical, not exhaustive:** A how-to guide does not need to cover everything. Start and end at meaningful points that solve the immediate problem, and avoid adding extra material that distracts from the goal.

- **Uses clear, user-oriented titles:** The title should state exactly what the guide delivers. "How to integrate application performance monitoring" is clear; "Application performance monitoring" is vague and could mean anything.

- **Addresses the reader directly:** Speak to the user as "you" to make the guide personal and actionable. Use conditional imperatives ("If you want X, do Y") to frame steps around their intent, reinforcing that the guide is about their project, not just what the tool can do.

Table 5-2 summarises the key differences between tutorials and how-to guides at a glance.

Table 5-2. *Comparison between Tutorials and How-to Guides*

Aspect	Tutorial	How-to Guide
Purpose	Teach by guiding through a practical project	Help achieve a goal as efficiently as possible
Audience	Beginners or those new to a concept/tool	Users with some familiarity who need to complete a task
Scope	Broader; covers concepts, tools, and skills	Narrow; focuses on one clearly defined outcome
Path	May include detours to teach concepts	Only the most direct route to success
Tone	Supportive, "we" language, hand-holding	Direct, concise, minimal narrative
Outcome	Knowledge and confidence	Completed task
Time to complete	Longer, often 20+ minutes	Short, 2–10 minutes
Example in cooking	"Learn to make a three-course Italian dinner"; teaches knife skills, cooking techniques, and timing	"How to make lasagna"; assumes you already know basic cooking skills

Reference Guides

Reference guides are often the most-used part of a documentation once
developers have moved past onboarding. They supports **Retention** in
the AARRRP framework by helping existing users deepen usage without
getting blocked, and **Activation** by giving new users a reliable source of
truth. Poor reference forces developers to guess, search Stack Overflow,
or inspect source code, all of which erode trust in your product's
documentation.

A strong reference entry is like a dictionary definition or a well-organized technical spec: it should be precise, complete, and unambiguous. The developer should not have to read the entire page to find the one detail they need.

Reference is for answering *"what is…?"* and *"how does it work?"* in a factual, comprehensive way. It is not the place to teach concepts or walk through workflows. It serves the application of skill, but unlike a how-to guide, it does not tell you what to do or in what order. It is there to answer questions like

- "What parameters does this API endpoint accept?"

- "What are the valid values for this configuration key?"

- "What is the syntax for this command?"

A reference guide typically has these characteristics:

- **Organized for quick lookup:** Structure content so users can find what they need without having to read from top to bottom. Use clear headings, consistent ordering of sections, and predictable formatting for each type of entry.

- **Complete but concise:** Cover all possible parameters, options, or elements, but keep descriptions short and to the point. Do not explain how to use them in context—link to a tutorial or how-to for that.

- **Accurate and up-to-date:** Reference is only valuable if it reflects the current behavior of the system. Out-of-date or incorrect values are worse than missing documentation because they mislead the user.

- **Factual, not instructional:** State what is true, not what to do. "The timeout value is in milliseconds" belongs here; "Set the timeout to 5000 for best results" belongs in a how-to guide.

- **Consistent formatting:** Use the same patterns, labels, and ordering across all reference entries so users can scan and compare quickly. For example, list parameters in alphabetical order, always specify default values, and present examples in the same style.

- **Searchable and linkable:** Each reference item should have a stable URL and be easy to navigate directly from search results.

Explanation Guides

Unlike tutorials, which guide learning through action, or how-to guides, which direct a task to completion, or reference material, which records precise facts, explanation steps back. Its perspective is higher and wider, looking at the topic as a whole, drawing connections, offering history and rationale, and weighing alternatives. It joins things together into a coherent mental model.

Explanation supports both Activation and Retention in the AARRRP framework by reducing uncertainty and building trust. It turns feature knowledge into product understanding, helping developers make informed decisions about how and when to apply your technology.

Even though it is less urgent than tutorials or how-to guides, explanation is not a luxury. No practitioner of a craft can master it without a clear view of the underlying principles, history, and context.

Explanation answers questions like

- "Why was this design chosen?"

- "What trade-offs exist between these two approaches?"

- "How does this concept fit into the bigger picture?"

When applied to cooking, explanation contains no recipes, and it is not a reference list of ingredients. Instead, it explores food and cooking through science, history, and culture. It explains why we sear meat, why bread rises, and how culinary traditions evolved. It's not something you read while cooking, but it changes how you think and, ultimately, how you practice the craft.

After reading such a book, your technical skill in the kitchen may not change overnight, but your understanding will. And that deeper understanding will influence your decisions, your style, and your confidence every time you cook.

A well-written explanation has these characteristics:

- **Makes connections:** Links related ideas, even across different areas. Shows how concepts relate to one another and to external contexts.

- **Provides context:** Explains the "why": design decisions, historical background, constraints, and trade-offs.

- **Keeps a clear topical boundary:** Stays focused on the chosen subject. Avoids drifting into step-by-step instruction (tutorial/how-to territory) or raw factual listings (reference territory).

- **Admits opinion and perspective:** Acknowledges that there are different ways to see the same problem. Weighs alternatives, presents counter-examples, and explains reasoning.

- **Uses "about" framing:** Titles and structure should make it clear that the document is about a topic ("About user authentication" or "About database connection policies"), inviting reflection rather than action.

- **Balances breadth with depth:** Covers the topic enough to give a solid understanding, but avoids turning into an encyclopedic reference or exhaustive treatise.

Table 5-3 summarises the key differences between reference and explanation documentation.

Table 5-3. *Difference between Reference and Explanation*

	Reference	Explanation
Purpose	To provide precise, factual information the reader can consult quickly	To deepen understanding by giving context, rationale, and connections
Focus	Facts, definitions, syntax, configuration options, API endpoints, parameters, limits	Principles, concepts, relationships, trade-offs, historical background, reasoning
Tone	Objective, factual, terse	Reflective, discursive, sometimes opinionated
When used	In the middle of doing work, when you need to look something up	Away from immediate work, when you want to think about a topic and see the bigger picture
Example	"fetch(url, { method: 'POST' }) — sends an HTTP POST request. Parameters: url (string), method (string)… "	"POST is used to send data to a server, typically to create a resource. Unlike GET, which is idempotent, POST changes server state and often requires careful validation."
Analogy	A dictionary. You open it to look up the spelling or meaning of a word.	An essay about the history and evolution of the language that word comes from

Use Good Docs Templates to Streamline Writing

The Good Docs Project is a community-driven library of ready-to-use templates for common documentation types. Where Diátaxis helps you decide *what kinds of documentation to write* and *how they fit together,*

Good Docs ensures you never have to start from a blank page. It gives you a well-structured starting point, with headings, prompts, and style recommendations that match proven best practices for each doc type.

While Diátaxis is a framework for information architecture, Good Docs is a toolkit for execution. It bridges the gap between "we know we need a tutorial here" and "here's exactly how to write it in a way that's clear, complete, and consistent."

The Good Docs Project offers templates for a wide range of doc types, many of which map naturally to the four Diátaxis categories:

- **Tutorials**: API quickstart, Quickstart guide, Installation guide

- **How-to guides**: How-to, Troubleshooting, Logging guide

- **Reference**: API reference, Release notes, Style guide

Explanation: Overview, Explanation, Code of conduct, Our Team page These templates are more than skeletons. They include recommended section orders, example phrasing, and reminders to include critical metadata such as last-updated dates, author names, and version numbers. You can check out the templates here.

With the good docs template, you'd be getting the benefits of

- **Faster production of new docs**: You skip the blank-page problem. Instead of figuring out from scratch how to organize a release note or quickstart, you follow a proven structure and adapt it to your context.

- **Consistent tone, style, and metadata**: Whether your docs are written by a DevRel lead, a support engineer, or a product manager, templates help maintain the same voice, formatting, and completeness across the documentation set.

- **Easier for users (and AI) to navigate and parse**:
  Consistency benefits not just human readers but
  also AI systems. Structured docs make it easier for
  large language models to extract accurate answers,
  match queries to the right section, and return clear,
  contextually correct responses.

  AI chat boxes will increasingly become the way
  developers consume documentation. Templates
  enforce that structure. They make sure terminology
  is consistent, that each doc contains all the necessary
  context, and that related content is linked logically—
  all of which improves AI retrieval and the accuracy of
  generated answers.

Apply Both Frameworks to Your Own Documentation

Once you have a clear understanding of the Diátaxis framework and the
Good Docs templates, the next step is applying them together to improve
your documentation in a structured and sustainable way.

Audit What You Have and Spot Gaps

This process begins with taking stock of what you already have and
identifying where the gaps are. Sometimes this is prompted by a
specific goal, such as an OKR to improve retention or activation, where
documentation has been identified as a bottleneck. Other times, the
need becomes clear through repeated user feedback, like questions that
keep resurfacing in support tickets, Slack threads, conference hallway
conversations, or GitHub issues.

Ideally, you should start with walking through your own quick start
guide as if you were a new developer. Do not skip steps, do not rely on your
insider knowledge. Note every point where you have to pause, make an

158

assumption, or leave the docs to search elsewhere. Better yet, watch a new developer try it, either live or via screen recording.

Then, review your documentation one page at a time. For each page

- Identify its intended category and purpose.

- Determine if it is a tutorial, a how-to guide, a reference, or an explanation.

- If it's trying to do too many things at once, split it into smaller, focused pieces and publish each under the correct category. This not only makes it easier for readers to find the right information but also improves the clarity and maintainability of the documentation.

Gaps often emerge during this process. You might discover, for example, that there is no clear explanation for a frequently asked "why" question, or that a key "how do I" workflow has never been documented. This is when you decide what type of documentation is needed. As a rule of thumb, listening for patterns in user questions also helps pinpoint the type of documentation required:

- "How do I…?" → Missing how-to guide.

- "What is…?" → Missing reference.

- "Why does…?" → Missing explanation.

- "Can you teach me…?" → Missing tutorial.

Table 5-4 maps common developer questions to the documentation type they signal is missing.

Table 5-4. *How Developer needs match to Documentation types*

User need or question type	Documentation type	Example
Learning + Action	Tutorial	"How do I integrate your SDK into a blank project?"
Application + Action	How-to Guide	"How do I migrate my database schema using your CLI?"
Application + Understanding	Reference	"What are the valid parameters for this API call?"
Learning + Understanding	Explanation	"Why does your framework use optimistic concurrency?"

Decide on Structure

Once you have identified what's missing or what needs improvement, the next step is to decide which documentation category each piece belongs to and see if there is a Good Docs template you can adopt.

Using a standardized template means you're never starting from a blank page, and you automatically follow a structure that improves readability for both humans and AI systems. Consistent structure, terminology, and formatting make it easier for AI tools to surface relevant answers, and for developers to scan and navigate your documentation.

Good Docs templates also encourage scannability by

- Opening with a clear first line that states exactly what the page covers

- Using headings and subheadings so readers can confirm relevance at a glance

- Including lateral links to related content, so users can move directly to what they need next

You can even integrate these templates into your documentation workflow so they auto-generate whenever a new page is created. For example, a script could prompt authors to pick the doc type, then pre-fill a markdown file with the correct sections from the template.

Once a page is written, decide where it fits in your overall information architecture. This is where Diátaxis shines. Look at Ubuntu's documentation: each product has its own landing page, and within it, all content is grouped into the four Diátaxis categories, as shown in Figure 5-3.

Figure 5-3. *Ubuntu Core Documentation showing usage of Diataxis*

Or see how Divio does it: tutorials are grouped under "Get Started" with separate tracks for different programming languages, feature explanations are collected under "Features," and conceptual pieces live in their own "Explanation" section, as shown in Figure 5-4.

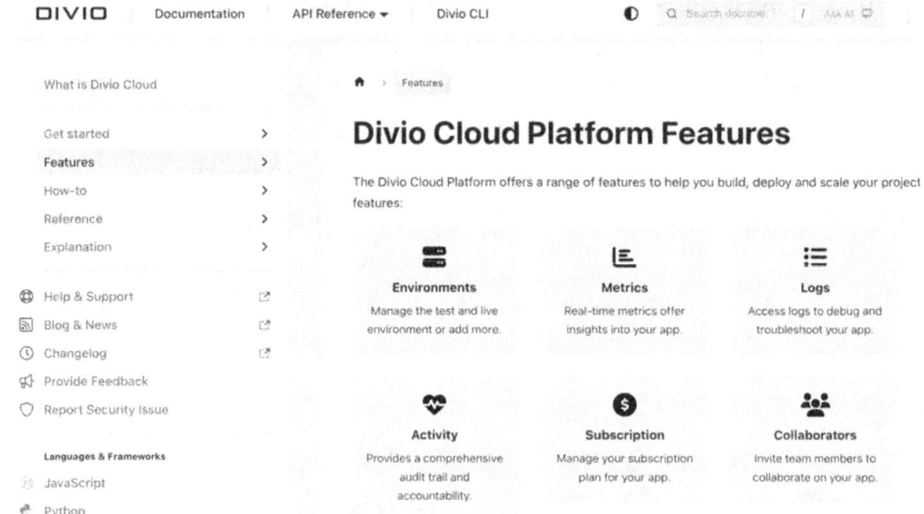

Figure 5-4. *Divio Documentation showing usage of Diataxis*

You don't need to copy these examples exactly. The goal is to create a structure that feels natural for your product, while making it clear to both users and writers where each new piece of content belongs.

Prioritize Critical Paths First

Once you know where each page belongs and how it will be written, you need to decide what to tackle first. Documentation work can quickly become overwhelming if you try to fix everything at once, so focus on changes that will deliver the greatest impact to your developers and your business goals.

A practical way to do this is to prioritize by *critical paths* which are the most common and important tasks your audience needs to complete successfully. You can find these by

- Reviewing analytics to see which pages get the most traffic or have the highest exit rates

- Looking at support tickets, community threads, and onboarding feedback to see where users get stuck

- Talking to sales engineers, developer advocates, or support teams to identify common "showstopper" issues

Score each task or topic based on its likelihood of being used to complete a critical path. For example:

- 3 = Very likely to be part of a critical path

- 2 = Sometimes relevant to key workflows

- 1 = Rarely needed for primary tasks

Tackle the highest-scoring items first. Often these will be

- Tutorials that unlock first success for new users.

- How-to guides that unblock a common production workflow.

- Reference pages for frequently used APIs or commands.

- Explanations for confusing concepts that repeatedly slow down adoption.

When scheduling the work, be realistic about your capacity. Break large updates into smaller, publishable improvements rather than waiting for a perfect, fully reworked doc set. Use time allocations to keep momentum. Say you have three weeks to document a feature, you can divide the time like so:

- Planning: 20% of the time

- Drafting: 50%

- Reviewing and editing: 20%

- Publishing: 10%

Protect Quality with Reviews, Automation, and Feedback

Lastly, treat your documentation with the same care and discipline as you treat your code. Store it in version control. Require peer review from at least one or two team members through pull requests. Keep reusable content in modular components so that updating one instance automatically updates all instances. Automate routine maintenance such as link checking, snippet testing, and version updates. These practices not only maintain quality but also reduce the long-term cost of keeping your documentation accurate and reliable.

Also consider setting up a feedback mechanism on every documentation page so users can share what's working and what's not in the moment. This can be as simple as a "Was this page helpful?" form with a comment box. Route all submissions to a dedicated documentation Slack channel where the relevant stakeholders are present.

Triaging this feedback weekly keeps issues from piling up and ensures nothing important slips through the cracks. Patterns in the feedback can signal structural problems (e.g., too much explanation in a how-to guide) or highlight missing content entirely.

5.2.6 Videos

This section is based on a conversation with Olayinka Oshidipe, an accomplished developer relations engineer. Olayinka has become one of the most recognized faces and voices in developer video content, particularly in the crypto space, where his 90-second demos and explainer videos have reached hundreds of thousands of developers worldwide. Many of his videos have gone viral on X shaping how new developers discover tools in a fast-moving ecosystem. His track record makes him a leading example of how short-form video can transform DevRel impact. As such, there was nobody better to co-author this section with.

Our discussion reinforced a simple truth. Video is no longer optional. It should be a core part of every developer relations strategy. With the rise of AI tools like ChatGPT and Perplexity, fewer developers rely on Google for informational queries. Many now get answers directly from these tools, which means the chance of them finding your blog through search is lower than it once was. The strongest way to reach developers today is to publish content directly on the platforms they already use and open every day.

This is why video has to be a core part of your developer advocacy strategy. YouTube, TikTok, Instagram, and X are where people instinctively spend time learning, laughing, and exploring, and developers are no different. Video on these platforms meets them where they are.

There are also so many other reasons why videos should be a non-negotiable for your strategy:

Video builds trust and connection. Developers often choose tools not just because they are technically superior, but because they feel "cooler" thanks to consistent and intentional storytelling. Tools like Supabase, Linear, or Superhuman have cultivated this effect, positioning themselves as aspirational choices even when competing with incumbents. Developers want more than dry technical details; they want to see the human side of a product. Faces, voices, and stories create emotional resonance. That connection turns viewers into advocates and strengthens loyalty within the community.

Video also boosts comprehension by making complex topics accessible. Seeing a product in action makes explanations clearer, and the combination of visual and auditory cues helps developers remember and apply concepts more effectively. Many technical features are difficult to explain through text alone, but video offers a way to walk through ideas step by step, creating a more immersive and compelling experience. This heightened engagement leads to better understanding, stronger retention, and ultimately more effective knowledge transfer.

Finally, video is powerful because it operates on a higher bandwidth than language. A person can read about 270 words per minute, which translates to roughly 12 bytes per second. Vision, by contrast, processes about 20 megabytes per second. Put differently, the data bandwidth of visual perception is over a million times higher than that of written or spoken language. This raw difference in capacity explains why video is such a compelling medium. It simply moves more information, faster, and in richer forms.

However, video is not a replacement for written content. Developer videos should rely on existing strong documentation. While video is critical, it should be treated as a complement or embed that extends reach, boosts engagement, and accommodates different learning needs and stages; Long-form YouTube tutorials or recorded talks for the implementation stage featuring deep explanations, step-by-step builds, and interactive demos. And, short-form formats on TikTok, Instagram, or YouTube Shorts for reach and awareness. Visual is maybe better for effectiveness, but written is better for longevity, referencing, and search retrieval. Both should work hand in hand. A 90-second demo or teaser cannot teach everything, but it can spark intrigue, encourage exploration, and direct viewers to your documentation or longer guides.

How to Do Videos Well

Olayinka breaks down his video-producing process into 5 steps, which typically takes him a full week to complete:

Research

Research is always the first step in creating developer video content, because it defines everything that comes after: the hook, the framing, even the editing style. Before you touch a script or camera, you need clarity on what stage of the developer journey your video is meant to serve. Are you aiming for awareness? If so, is it awareness for developers who already recognize the problem space, or for those who are unaware of the space but live with an unrealized problem your product solves? Each audience requires a different entry point.

Awareness videos that do well anchor themselves to conversations developers are already having. That could be a new Ethereum proposal, a popular thread on Twitter, or a GitHub issue gaining traction. The task is to pay attention to what developers recognize instantly and use it as the opening door.

If you notice developers asking about scaling NextJS APIs or comparing React to other frameworks, you can build a video that starts from that conversation and positions your product as part of the answer. For instance, there was a time when NestJS was trending, you might frame your video as *"How to build a full-stack app with NestJS using [your product]"* or *"React vs NestJS for X task."* By starting with a reference point they instantly recognize, you can then guide them toward what they actually need to know and show, step by step, how your product solves the problem.

When you've decided on a trend or angle to frame your video around, that's when you now start researching details to build context for your script.

Scripting

After research comes the hard part: distilling only what is truly needed into a script. For Olayinka, who focuses on 90-second short-form videos, this is the most important phase, often taking two to four days. The challenge is deciding what can realistically fit into that limited time frame. It starts with asking, what is the single most important takeaway worth amplifying, and what can be left for follow-up or the comments? This careful filtering sets the stage for scripting, where raw research is transformed into a story.

For Olayinka, here is the flow he usually follows for short explainer videos:

1. **Hook**: Open with something instantly familiar or trending so the right developers lean in. Example: "You've heard the buzz about account abstraction. Here's what actually changed."

2. **Intro**: State what the video covers in one clean sentence.

3. **Establish the topic**: Define the concept in simple, precise language.

4. **Context**: Recap prior attempts or predecessors and why they fell short. Example: "Earlier proposals solved parts of the problem but created friction for wallets."

5. **Core explanation**: Show what is new or how your approach solves the problem.

6. **Wrap-up**: Give the takeaway and the next click, usually a link to your docs or a longer demo.

This isn't a one-size-fits-all. There are several other effective storytelling structures that you can use for your explainers. For short-form tutorials, though, the rhythm changes. Developers who click into a tutorial already have intent, so you skip the hook-heavy setup and go straight to the walkthrough giving them immediate visual progress: "Create a Next.js project, install the SDK, and deploy."

While scripting, you want to make sure that you use short sentences instead of long ones. Each thought should stand as a beat the editor can cut to. Try reading the script out loud; if a phrase makes you stumble, it will make viewers stumble too. Keep the language conversational and exact, trimming anything that feels like "nice to know" rather than "need to know."

You should also weave in humor and entertainment to leave a lasting impression. For longer-form content, humor can be verbalized directly. For shorter-form content where every word and second matters, Olayinka advises introducing humor and entertainment through cutaways, memes, or sound cues.

Filming/Recording

Once the script is ready, the next hurdle is recording. You want to make sure that your delivery feels natural and full of charisma. If your delivery is awkward, viewers will likely drop off. Being comfortable in front of a camera may not come naturally, and that is okay. With practice, you can improve.

One effective approach is to record draft versions of your script that will never be published. Watch them back to get comfortable with your own voice and body language. Over time, the repetition chips away at the awkwardness. What feels forced at first will start to look natural, and the more comfortable you appear on camera, the more at ease your viewers will feel watching you.

When it comes to delivery, there are several approaches, and each comes with trade-offs. Reading from a teleprompter ensures accuracy, but the result often feels stiff and overly rehearsed. Full improvisation can feel authentic and conversational, but it risks rambling, bloated takes, and wasted time in retakes. The middle ground is usually the most effective: memorize your script section by section, then deliver it in manageable chunks. This balance gives you the structure needed to stay concise while leaving room for natural asides, emphasis, or humor that add personality.

As a general rule, longer videos benefit from a teleprompter to keep you on track, while shorter videos are sharper when memorized, since they require more punch and energy.

Christian Heilmann built a script prompter that I quite like: `https://codepo8.github.io/prompter`. Each paragraph from your script will be displayed as a big font on top of the screen for you to read.

That way you can read it and still look straight into the camera.

Technical setup matters, but it does not have to be extravagant. As at the time of writing this, Olayinka's go-to gear includes a Sony ZV-E10 camera paired with a Sigma 31.4 lens, lit by a Godox SL60W with a softbox.

For audio, he uses a Hollyland Lark M2 microphone and cleans the track with AI tools during postproduction. That said, excellent videos can still be produced with more modest equipment, even an iPhone with the Blackmagic Camera App, as long as you nail the fundamentals: clear audio, strong lighting, and an uncluttered, symmetrical set. If you must prioritize, start with good audio. Viewers will forgive imperfect visuals long before they forgive distorted or unclear sound.

The awesome DevRel repository on GitHub also has some awesome community-sourced content creation tooling recommendations here: `https://github.com/devrelcollective/awesome-devrel`

Interestingly, the rise of AI video generator tools is already giving us a glimpse at a future where filming might become a totally optional or unnecessary stage of video creation. Tools such as Pictory and Vyond can take a script and automatically generate full videos with visuals, b-roll, music, and animations for videos like product explainers, announcements, or quick how-tos.

And for cases where a human presence is valuable, platforms like HeyGen and Arogil can now create avatars that mimic realistic facial expressions, gestures, and multiple camera angles, even cloning the creator's likeness. Although, at the time of writing this, these avatars still have limitations, with audio often out of sync or gestures feeling unnatural. But they offer a glimpse of a future where DevRel teams can produce high-quality videos quickly without needing heavy equipment or on-camera talent.

Editing

Editing is the stage where everything comes together. It is what turns a plain recording into something polished and engaging. This is also where you introduce rhythm. Viewers lose focus quickly if the scene stays static for too long. Changing the frame, adding movement, or introducing a new element every five to ten seconds helps reset attention and keeps the audience watching.

Editing is also where humor and creativity come in. Memes, GIFs, sound effects, or motion graphics can lift a straightforward explanation into something that feels alive. Small touches like on-screen notes, fly-ins, or knowledge checks give viewers more than words to follow and make the video feel interactive rather than passive.

It is also the stage where you adapt your video for different platforms. On YouTube, adding chapters makes it easier for developers to jump directly to the sections they care about. On LinkedIn, captions are important because videos autoplay without sound. On TikTok, Instagram Reels, or Shorts, shorter clips with faster cuts perform better. Tailoring edits for each platform ensures the same content reaches further.

Many DevRel teams outsource editing. Olayinka does this to save time and keep his focus on research, scripting, and delivery, which only he can do as the subject matter expert. Outsourcing raises quality while freeing up creative energy for the parts of the process that need it most.

If outsourcing is not an option, for any reason, there are still resources to help. YouTube is filled with tutorials that teach the basics of pacing, transitions, and sound design. Sites like Spectacle.is provide a deep library of inspiration, showcasing how brands across industries use video—from product explainers to customer stories to quick social clips. Studying these examples can give you templates and ideas for an editing style that feels professional and on-brand without requiring years of experience.

Publishing and Retrospectives

After your video is ready, approaching publishing with consistency is just as important as the content itself. A regular cadence builds trust and even creates anticipation. Olayinka, for instance, releases his videos every Friday at 6:30 p.m., a slot he chose because it overlaps with multiple global time zones, giving his videos a strong first four hours of visibility.

Your schedule may look different, but the key is to commit to one and stick with it. Over time, that reliability builds momentum and sets an expectation with your audience.

But publishing is not the finish line. Each release is also an experiment. To grow in the craft, you need retrospectives. Observe analytics and pay attention to where viewers drop off, when reactions spike, and which hooks land best. These signals reveal how your pacing, storytelling, and framing resonate. Some videos will underperform, others will spark conversation or adoption. Both outcomes are useful data.

When you find something that works, audit it closely. Break down what made it effective, and then capture those lessons in a repeatable template. Instead of starting from scratch each time, you'll build a playbook of narrative flows and techniques that you can adapt across formats. The process of consistent publishing and deliberate reflection compounds, sharpening your instincts and making every new video stronger than the last.

5.3 Designing Your Content for Discovery and Scale

You've read best practices for executing different content formats. You've also learned how to scale and improve your workflow using AI tools. But you don't have to do it all.

Except in very big intercontinental companies, most Developer Relations teams are small, often fewer than ten people. That means your capacity is limited, so you need to pick wisely, start focused, and scale methodically. The best way to do this is to choose a primary content format and build your systems around it. Create once, then multiply your impact through smart repurposing and distribution.

5.3.1 Pick a Primary Format You Can Win With

Your primary format will depend on a few things:

- Where your target developer personas go to solve problems

- What format aligns with the developer journey stage you're creating for

- What format you're likely to see the most wins with, given your team's capabilities and your company's goals

Many DevRel teams default to blogs as their primary format. It makes sense. Writing scales, and has long been a superb way to reach developers anywhere in the world. But that strategy was built for a time when Google was the main way people discovered information. But as I teased in the video section, that's no longer the case. Picking blog articles as your core format for awareness, acquisition, activation, and retention deserves a rethink.

The rise of AI tools like ChatGPT and Perplexity has changed how people search for information. Developers now turn to these tools for fast, aggregated answers—especially for informational queries, which are exactly the kind DevRel teams tend to target. Instead of searching "how to partition a SQL table" on Google, many developers now ask ChatGPT directly and never click through to a website.

Even when people do use Google, 60% of searches end without a single click, according to research from SparkToro. This is especially true for informational searches. Users looking for branded, transactional, or navigational results—like "buy Nike shoes" or "MongoDB pricing page"—are still more likely to click. But for top-of-funnel educational content, Google is no longer the discovery engine it once was.

That's why it may make more sense to prioritize content platforms developers open on their own, without needing to search. These are platforms they browse for fun, for updates, or to learn something new. YouTube, LinkedIn, and Reddit often fit this pattern. Some younger developers are building similar habits with TikTok, though you'll want to assess whether the platform fits your audience and goals.

Most developers do not wake up and type in your blog URL. But they do open YouTube, scroll LinkedIn, or read Reddit regularly. That's probably where your awareness efforts should begin.

5.3.2 Create Once, Repurpose Many Times

Once you've committed to a format and shipped something valuable, make sure you get the most out of it. Choosing a primary format doesn't mean other formats are off the table. It just means you start with one and then build a repeatable system for repurposing and distributing your content across other formats and channels.

Max Katz (`https://maxkatz.net/`), who previously worked at IBM, shared how his team does this well. They host at least one online event—usually a webinar or online meetup—every week. Each event is recorded, edited, and uploaded to YouTube. From there, they create a blog post to accompany the video, embedding it alongside a short description of what was covered.

Most online events include a Q&A session. Some of the answers might be rushed or brief due to time limits. In some cases, you might not have a solid answer in the moment. After the event, IBM's team collects all those questions and publishes a follow-up blog post with detailed responses, including answers to any questions they couldn't tackle live. If the event included a workshop, they might take the workshop steps and turn them into a stand-alone tutorial. That's another valuable piece of content.

In the end, this approach turns one event into multiple content assets: a YouTube video, a blog post, a detailed Q&A, and a tutorial.

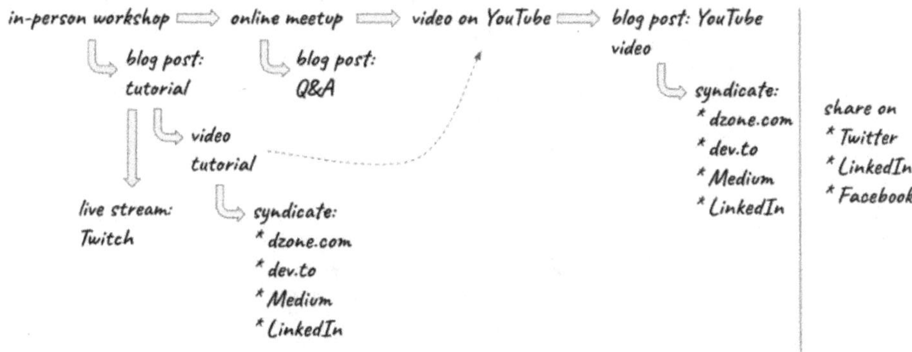

Figure 5-5. *Online Event Repurposing Workflow illustrating how one event can generate multiple content assets across formats and channels, extending reach and lifespan*

Your flow might look different. Maybe you start by answering questions on Reddit, then create a video to expand on one of those answers. That video can become a blog post with the embedded video, followed by a community talk or even a podcast episode.

The point is, don't just publish a webinar, blog post, or video and move on. Excellent content ideas are hard to come by. You should maximize the value of each one.

And when I say not to make blogs your primary format, I don't mean you should stop writing blog posts. In fact, more and more LLMs now cite blogs as sources, which can drive traffic to your site. When I was at Smallstep, we started to see an uptick in referrals coming directly from ChatGPT.

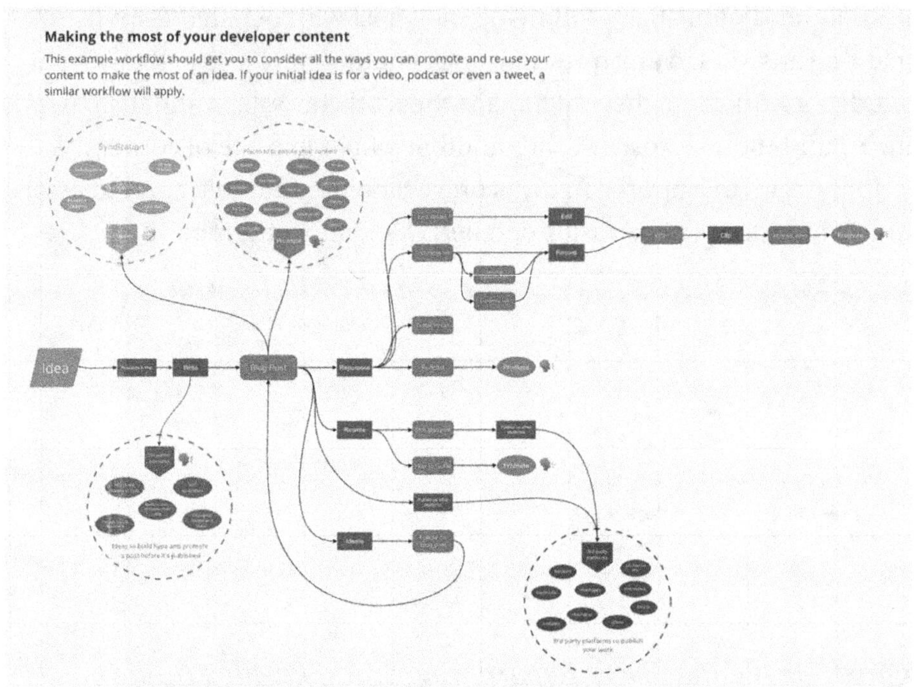

*Figure 5-6   Content Repurposing Workflow put together by
CodingWithRyan*

5.3.3 Distribute and Promote Like Your Life Depends on It

Even the best content fails if no one sees it. Distribution is not an
afterthought. It is half the work. You need systems for getting your content
in front of developers, on the platforms they already trust.

Great content gets you seen once. A strong distribution engine gets
you seen again and again, by the right people, at scale. Relying solely on
organic discovery is no longer enough.

Start with email. Share new content in your newsletter. Post it in your community Slack. Ask your team to share it on LinkedIn, ideally adding their own thoughts. Employee advocacy works. People trust people more than brands. Executives, in particular, often have large followings. You can ghostwrite a post or collaborate with them to shape a thoughtful message. Don't rely solely on the brand handle.

Reach out to developer influencers or advocates who might want to reference or reshare it. For broader reach, republish on platforms like Dev.to or Medium using canonical links. Explore cross-promotions with parallel companies that speak to the same audience.

AI tools can help recap content for various platforms, but remember that each one has its own best practices. A post that performs well on Reddit may flop on LinkedIn. Take the time to optimize content for each channel. And never just drop a link. Social platforms downrank link-based posts, and users rarely engage with them. Instead, adapt the message. Share a quote. Summarize a story. Add a visual. Or ask a provocative question.

Williams from Red Hat found that for his team

- Twitter worked best for links with strong descriptions.

- Facebook favored code snippets.

- LinkedIn thrived on professional or educational content.

- Reddit needed strong, clear opinions to spark discussion.

You'll succeed when you make distribution a habit by building it into your team's workflow. Every week during your team standup, pick a fresh piece of content—ideally one connected to a campaign—and repurpose it together. Draft copy for multiple platforms (e.g., Hacker News, Reddit, LinkedIn, and X), review it as a group, and schedule posts. Create multiple versions so you can reshare the same content 2–3 times spaced over weeks with new framing. **T**ools like Buffer, HubSpot, or SproutSocial can help to manage the queue.

Don't forget to respond to comments and join the conversation. And send to customer-facing teams (sales, support, success, or marketing) so they can include them in their newsletters.

Summary

Turning a DevRel plan into reality depends on how well you create and deliver content that speaks to developers' actual needs. The most effective material goes beyond information sharing. It solves problems, meets developers at the right stage of their journey, and respects how they prefer to consume knowledge. A practical tutorial, a skimmable blog post, or a well-paced webinar can all build trust when chosen with care.

But, creation alone is not enough. For content to have lasting impact, it must be distributed intentionally. A consistent cadence across channels, combined with smart repurposing, extends the lifespan of a single idea. Sharing it in different formats, tailoring it for each platform, and amplifying it through colleagues or community champions ensures the work keeps reaching new audiences instead of vanishing after one release.

At its core, execution is about alignment. Every blog post, video, or community program should trace back to the goals you set earlier: business priorities, developer needs, and the story you want to tell about the product. When you connect those dots consistently, advocacy becomes not only effective but repeatable.

In the next chapter, we shift the lens from outward-facing work to inward impact: how to measure success, interpret feedback, and prove that advocacy is driving results.

CHAPTER 6

Measuring the Impact and Success of Your Developer Advocacy Efforts with Metrics

In the previous chapters, we explored how to define your strategic focus and choose the right bets, whether that's tutorials, docs, or events. But shipping those things isn't the end goal. You also need to know if your work is helping developers and moving the business forward.

For a long time, the phrase "DevRel is hard to measure" was used as both an excuse and a kind of protective shield. It was a short-sighted attempt at protecting the authenticity of the work.

Developer Relations is built on trust. Advocates need to be seen as genuine peers, not salespeople in disguise. The fear was that if you applied sales or marketing style KPIs to advocacy (which was usually the case in uninformed companies), you'd flatten the nuance of what advocates do—reducing a relationship-driven craft to a numbers game—and in doing so, strip them of credibility with developers.

© Linda Ikechukwu 2026
L. Ikechukwu, *A Friendly Guide to Developer Advocacy*, Friendly Guides to Technology,
https://doi.org/10.1007/979-8-8688-2462-3_6

But here's the hard truth: avoiding measurement is exactly why DevRel is often one of the first teams cut when layoffs come. When budgets tighten, functions that cannot explain their impact are always the most vulnerable. Authenticity and credibility do not have to be sacrificed on the altar of metrics. Even rock stars need to sell tickets if they want to keep touring. Influencers have to deliver results if they want to be invited back to campaigns.

The work may be creative, human, and relationship-based, but it still has to connect to outcomes that matter to the company. If you make metrics your ally, they become both your defense against doubt and your lever for growth. By keeping a disciplined handle on measurement, you can

- Prove your value to leadership

- See whether your current strategy is working, and pivot when needed

- Strengthen your case when negotiating for resources, promotions, or expanding your work

This chapter demystifies metrics for developer advocacy, gives you a toolkit to choose meaningful ones, and tie them back to company goals to tell a story that executives understand.

That said, this chapter does not discuss how to source metrics or attribution data using any specific tool, because tools abound and are constantly evolving. Rather, it provides a framework for how to think about metrics, settled on from my own experience and what others have had to say about the topic. It's not something you have to follow to a T, but it's one I hope you find inspiration from.

6.1 What Not to Do When Picking Your Metrics

When picking metrics to track or report on, you need to take care that you don't make the following mistakes:

6.1.1 Don't Choose Metrics That Are Overly Complex to Collect

If it would take an army of BI engineers to implement such a complex report or require the necessity of close collaboration with three other departments, then you are setting yourself up for failure. The more complicated a metric is to collect, the harder it will be to keep up-to-date and the less useful it will be for making quick decisions.

A good metric should not require exotic infrastructure or weeks of setup to track. For example, if you want to understand whether your tutorials are driving product usage, you can look at referral traffic from blog posts to your documentation or trial sign-ups tied to specific content. That's manageable with existing tools. If, however, your metric requires stitching together your CRM, analytics, marketing automation platform, and finance systems just to spit out one quarterly number, you will spend more time wrangling data than acting on insights.

6.1.2 Don't Choose Untrusted Metrics

It's not enough that the metrics you choose can be measured. They also need to be **trusted metrics** that other teams and executives can immediately associate with business impact. If you put your metric in front of a VP, CEO, or Product Manager and they need a 15-minute explanation to understand it, it's time to reevaluate your approach.

A trusted metric is one the company already accepts as a valid measure of success. These are typically quantitative, directly tied to revenue or cost, and standardized across departments or industries. They are the language executives, finance, and product teams use to evaluate business performance. They include

- Annual Recurring Revenue (ARR)

- Monthly Active Users (MAUs)

- Conversion rate

- Churn

- Customer Acquisition Cost (CAC)

- Customer Lifetime Value (LTV), etc.

These metrics are trusted because they sit close to the company's North Star metric, which is the single metric that best captures the core value your product delivers. I talk about North Star metrics more in the next section.

The closer your DevRel metrics are to that North Star, the more trusted it is, and the easier it becomes for others to see their business value.

For instance, "% increase in the percentage of developers who complete onboarding within their first week" instantly communicates value. Everyone understands what onboarding means and why time-to-value matters for adoption and retention.

Compare that to metrics like "normalized weighted engagement score by developer persona across multiple channels," "community sentiment improved by 20%," or "positive feedback from Discord." These may signal progress, but they do not communicate anything concrete about adoption, retention, or revenue. And, without a clear link to business outcomes or proof of impact, they remain untrusted and irrelevant to the C-suite.

One of the easiest ways to make your abstract DevRel metrics more
trusted is demonstrating how your work influences the company's most
trusted indicators. For example, rather than just reporting "documentation
satisfaction improved," you report

- When documentation satisfaction increased from 60%
  to 85%, activation rates rose by 12%.

- Community-led support reduced ticket volume by 18%,
  saving $45,000 in quarterly support costs.

- Developers who participated in workshops were 30%
  more likely to convert to active users.

This is the kind of proof that translates abstract DevRel outcomes
directly into concrete business outcomes that executives understand,
making your metrics trusted and your function indispensable.

6.1.3 Don't Fall into the Vanity Metrics Trap

Vanity metrics are what top-of-funnel metrics become when they are
treated as proof of success.

At first glance, they look like progress. The numbers are going up.
The charts look healthy. It feels like momentum. But when these metrics
are tracked in isolation, they stop being signals and start becoming
distractions.

Top-of-funnel metrics answer a very specific question: are we
being seen?

They do not answer the harder questions that actually matter. Do
developers care enough to try the product? Do they trust it? Are they
succeeding with it? Is any of this creating downstream impact for the
business? They do not reveal where developers struggle, what blocks
adoption, or why people drop off before reaching success.

Common examples include

- Overall website traffic

- Blog page views

- Signups

- Organic traffic

- Brand awareness

- Social media engagement

- Bounce rates

- Video clicks

- Click-through rates

These metrics are not inherently bad. They can tell you whether your work is reaching people. But reach alone is not progress.

Think about it. A viral tweet with hundreds of thousands of impressions may feel like a win. But if none of those impressions lead to developers downloading your SDK, integrating your API, or shipping something real, what did that spike actually create? You captured attention, but you did not move your mission forward?

This is what makes the vanity metrics trap dangerous. Top-of-funnel numbers are easy to inflate. Under pressure, teams start optimizing for what looks good on a dashboard. Want more page views? Write clickbait headlines that attract curiosity but leave readers disappointed. Want more signups? Put useful content behind a login wall and watch registrations climb. Over time, strategy bends toward feeding the chart rather than serving the developer.

Instead of anchoring on top-of-funnel metrics that easily turn into vanity metrics, focus on actionable or success metrics.

Vanity metrics are indicators. Actionable metrics are outcomes. They show whether developers are making real progress with your product, not just glancing at it. They give you feedback you can act on and help you understand how developers move from first contact to real value.

Here are a few ways to reframe top-of-funnel numbers into actionable ones.

- Instead of counting only video views, also track the percentage of viewers who went on to complete onboarding within a week. If 10,000 people watched your tutorial, that looks great on paper. But if only 2% of them went on to try your product, that's a very different story. By reframing the metric to track how many viewers completed onboarding within a week, you shift the focus to a signal of real adoption.

- Instead of reporting only raw page views on docs, also measure time to first success. Page views don't tell you if your docs are effective. But measuring "time to first success"—the average time it takes for a developer to make their first successful API call after starting the quickstart—gives you a metric that reveals whether your documentation is doing its job. It highlights friction points, shows you where to improve, and most importantly, connects documentation directly to developer success.

- Instead of tracking only the number of product sign-ups, also look at the percentage who became active users within 30 days. A sign-up is not the same as an active user. Anyone can be forced through a registration form, but that doesn't mean they will return tomorrow. A more actionable measure is the percentage of sign-ups that became active users within 30 days. That figure shows whether your onboarding process, your product value, and your developer experience are strong enough to turn interest into sustained use.

Actionable metrics are usually smaller numbers, but they are far more useful. They replace feel-good dashboards with signals you can learn from. When you make this shift, you stop serving metrics and start serving developers.

The goal is not to abandon top-of-funnel measurement. It is to connect it to outcomes. When your metrics reflect behaviors that matter, like activation, retention, referrals, and expansion, you gain clarity on where your strategy is working and where it is falling short, as illustrated in Figure 6-1.

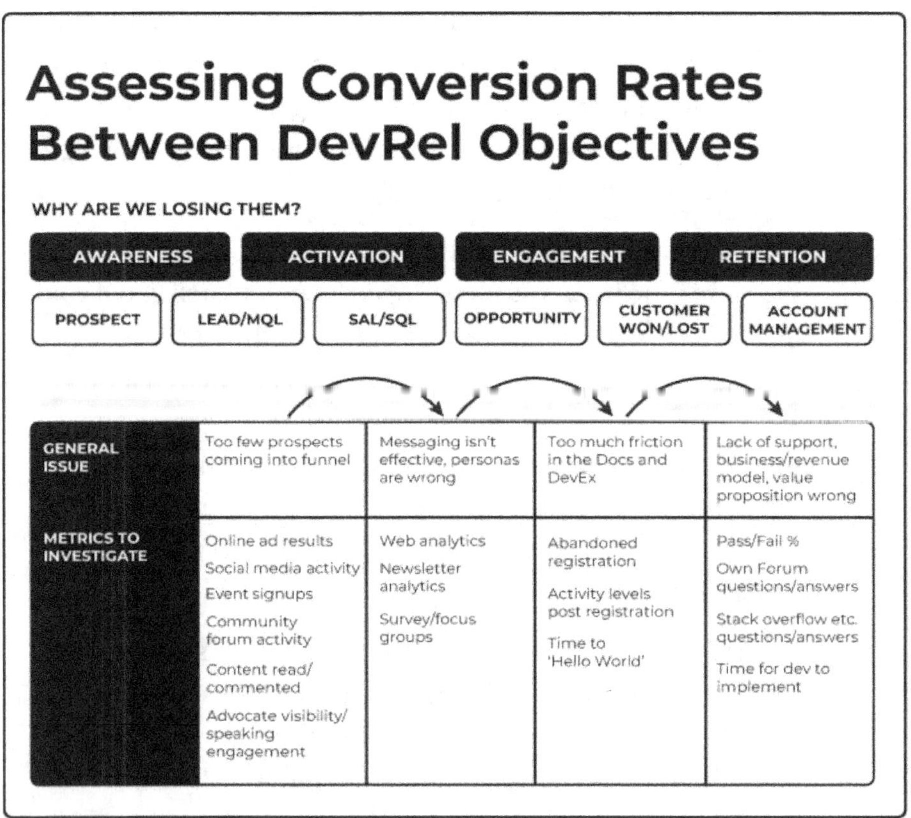

GENERAL ISSUE	Too few prospects coming into funnel	Messaging isn't effective, personas are wrong	Too much friction in the Docs and DevEx	Lack of support, business/revenue model, value proposition wrong
METRICS TO INVESTIGATE	Online ad results Social media activity Event signups Community forum activity Content read/commented Advocate visibility/speaking engagement	Web analytics Newsletter analytics Survey/focus groups	Abandoned registration Activity levels post registration Time to 'Hello World'	Pass/Fail % Own Forum questions/answers Stack overflow etc. questions/answers Time for dev to implement

Figure 6-1. A framework for diagnosing drop-offs across the DevRel funnel, using metrics specific to each stage of the developer journey. Originally created by Caroline Lewko and James Parton

6.2 What to Do When Picking Your Metrics

When it comes to metrics, there's no shortage of options. That abundance is precisely the trap.

One of the biggest mistakes teams make is drowning in numbers or tracking every possible data point until reporting becomes a full-time job. Metrics should guide valuable work, not replace it.

While the industry standard recommends tracking five to ten metrics, fewer is often better. Every metric you choose should tie directly to the company's goals and the core metrics the business already tracks. This may sound obvious, but many Developer Relations teams get it wrong. When your goals are not aligned with the company's broader objectives, your impact becomes invisible, and your work looks disconnected.

In Chapter 4, we discussed defining a strategic focus and OKRs based on company goals too. Once your strategic focus and OKRs are clear, your metrics should be designed to show measurable progress toward them.

There's no one-size-fits-all formula here. The right metrics vary with your company's goals, product maturity, and business model.

But here's what I'd advise:

6.2.1 Identify Your Company's North Star and Keystone Metrics

Before you can define Developer Relations metrics, you need to understand what the company itself measures success against.

Every organization has a North Star Metric, which is the single metric that captures the relationship between the value it delivers to users and the value it captures as a business.

The North Star metric is the one metric that shows whether users are getting sustained value from your product in a way that drives growth. Growth in the North Star Metric should reliably lead to growth in revenue or retention.

Based on that lens, here are reasonable examples of what that might look like for different companies:

- If you are Spotify, it is *time spent listening*, because that means users are finding consistent value in the music library.

- If you are Airbnb, it is *nights booked*, which shows that both sides of the marketplace—hosts and guests—are active and satisfied.

- If you are Slack, it is *messages sent within organizations*, which signals team engagement and long-term retention.

For most developer-focused companies, the North Star Metric is some variant of Monthly Active Developers (MADs) and/or Annual Recurring Revenue (ARR).

MADs reflect whether developers are consistently engaging with and deriving value from the product. ARR captures whether that engagement translates into sustained business value.

Beneath the North Star Metric are Keystone Metrics. These are more specific, measurable indicators that move the North Star forward. They capture the intermediate steps that signal progress toward sustainable usage or revenue. Examples include

- Registrations or signups

- Activations such as a first successful API call, SDK integration, or deployment

- Downloads or installations

- Deals closed

- Growth in deployed projects or active environments

Your company's keystone metrics depend on how they capture value. Some companies capture value through subscriptions. Others capture value through open-source adoption, enterprise contracts, or usage-based billing.

For example, for a self-serve SaaS company, revenue is typically usage-driven or subscription-based, so activation and retention matter most. Supporting Keystone Metrics might include

- Growth in signups or registrations

- Activated developers (those who complete a first successful task such as an API call or SDK integration after signup)

- Conversion rate from free to paid accounts

- Adoption rate of key activation features that correlate with higher conversion likelihood

For an open-source or hybrid company, open-source adoption drives the credibility and reach that later convert into paid support, enterprise licenses, or managed offerings. While the open-source community may not directly generate revenue, it expands the surface area for commercial opportunities.

In this case, keystone metrics could include

- Number of contributors or maintainers

- Frequency of commits or releases

- Package downloads

- Organizations integrating the project into production systems

For an enterprise, B2B, or sales-led company where revenue comes from large contracts or integrations, your keystone metrics might center on deals closed, proof-of-concept completions, or enterprise activations which tie directly to ARR and expansion revenue.

6.2.2 Pick a Primary DevRel Metric

Now that you understand your company's North Star and Keystone Metrics, the next step is to define your primary Developer Advocacy metric. This is the metric that demonstrates how your team's actions directly support or influence the company's Keystone Metric.

Let's revisit some example scenarios from Chapter 4.

Scenario: You're working at an early-stage company whose primary goal is to increase its user base by 30% and achieve a 20% growth in annual recurring revenue (ARR).

At this stage, the company is still building traction. It has product-market fit in sight but not fully achieved. The focus is on driving consistent adoption, validating core use cases, and converting early adopters into paying customers. The company's Keystone Metrics might include

- Growth in new developer signups or registrations

- Growth in activated developers (developers who complete a key product action such as an API call or SDK integration)

- Conversion rate from free to paid accounts

Your **primary DevRel metric** needs to demonstrate how your activities move those keystone metrics forward.

To do that, you can follow this thought process:

1. **Start from the company's Keystone Metric:** The company is tracking growth in new signups and ARR. These are the ultimate indicators of whether the business is expanding.

2. **Ask what DevRel can directly influence:** Developer Relations can't directly close sales or control revenue growth, but it can remove friction that slows

adoption. The strategic bets and OKRs we agreed on in Chapter 4 improve documentation, streamline onboarding, and help developers reach their first moment of success faster.

3. **Translate that influence into a clear, measurable outcome:** In this case, the goal is adoption. You want to show that more developers are not only discovering the product but also actively using it. Your primary metric could therefore be: *Number of signups or registrations originating from DevRel-owned channels and content (tracked through UTM in CTAs)*

Scenario: You're working at a scale-up company entering a new phase of growth. The company's primary goal for the quarter is to expand into new markets, such as EMEA.

At this stage, the business has already achieved some level of product-market fit. It's generating recurring revenue, has a stable user base, and now wants to replicate that success across regions. The company's *Keystone Metrics* might include

- Growth in new regional signups or activated developers (e.g., signups originating from EMEA)

- Market-specific ARR growth

- Regional adoption rate for localized versions, SDKs, or documentation

Again, your primary DevRel metric should show how your actions are accelerating that regional expansion with momentum in awareness, adoption, and advocacy within your target market.

Following the same thought process as the first scenario

1. **Start from the company's Keystone Metric:** The company is tracking growth in new signups and ARR from said regions which are the ultimate indicators of whether the expansion efforts are working.

2. **Ask what DevRel can directly influence:** Developer Relations cannot close enterprise deals directly, but it can influence and accelerate *market readiness*: building local awareness, reducing friction for new users, and equipping advocates who amplify adoption.

3. **Translate this influence into measurable actions that precede revenue:** The key is to pick the one that's most predictive of long-term adoption and revenue. For a scale-up entering new regions, a strong primary DevRel metric could be: *Number of activated developers in new markets (EMEA) within the quarter.*

In some cases, your company may also operate a sales-led organization in tandem with their self-service option, where their Keystone Metrics may also include *"**number of deals closed.**"*

In such environments, Marketing often reports on Marketing Qualified Leads (MQLs), that is, prospects who have shown interest through campaigns or website interactions and are deemed ready for outreach by Sales. Developer Relations can complement this system by defining Developer Relations Qualified Leads (DQLs) as part of its primary metrics.

A **Developer Relations Qualified Lead** is a variant of the traditional MQL framework introduced by Mary Thengvall and refers to a potential customer or partner identified through DevRel-owned channels and interactions. These leads are valuable because they combine technical credibility with authentic product interest.[1]

DQLs can be generated in two ways:

- **Directly:** Through DevRel campaigns such as newsletters, workshops, webinars, or tutorials that attract developers who register or request follow-up information.

- **Indirectly:** Through community interactions that signal strong product affinity. For instance, a developer who consistently answers questions in your forum, writes tutorials about your SDK, or contributes to your open-source repositories may be an excellent contact for Marketing or Sales.

Over time, tracking how many of these DevRel-qualified prospects enter the sales pipeline and eventually convert allows you to quantify Developer Relations' contribution to revenue. It also strengthens the narrative that advocacy is not just about awareness but about influencing real business outcomes.

6.2.3 Define Your Success Metrics

Your primary Developer Advocacy primary metrics connect directly to company-level impact. Your success metrics (otherwise known as activity metrics) help you understand why your primary metrics are either moving forward or not.

---

[1] Mary Thengvall, *DevRel Qualified Leads: Repurposing a Common Business Metric to Prove Value*, 2019 (`https://www.marythengvall.com/blog/2019/12/14/devrel-qualified-leads-repurposing-a-common-business-metrics-to-prove-value`)

Success metrics measure the health and performance of your activities or strategic bets. They tell you whether the strategic bets you chose are working as intended, or if you need to adjust your approach. You may include them in your executive report or not, but you need them to operate effectively as a team.

For example, let's revisit the early-stage company scenario where the goal is to grow the user base by 30% and increase ARR by 20%.

We decided that our strategic bets would focus on helping developers see value quickly through practical use cases, reducing onboarding friction by improving documentation, setup flows, and clarity around first success, and closing the feedback loop by channeling developer insights back to Product and communicating improvements back to users.

You're looking for quantifiable signs that your changes made developers more successful, faster. You're looking for evidence that onboarding improvements, better documentation, and user feedback are indeed the levers that unlock adoption and retention.

You might consider success metrics like

- **Time to first success:** Has the average time between signup and first API call, deployment, or integration decreased?

- **Content performance:** How are tutorials performing in traffic, views, or shares? What percentage of those viewers go on to sign up or activate?

- **Documentation satisfaction score:** What's the average rating of clarity or usefulness from feedback widgets or periodic surveys?

- **Onboarding completion rate:** What percentage of developers start and finish a quickstart after signing up?

- **Reduction in repetitive support tickets:** Are you seeing fewer recurring "how-to" questions after improving your docs?

- **Churn rate reduction:** Are fewer developers going inactive after onboarding or feature improvements driven by community feedback?

After a few months, it's time to check whether your assumptions hold true. Sometimes, the data agrees with your hypothesis. Other times, it tells a different story, like

1. **Signups drop while activation rises:** You fixed onboarding, but fewer new developers are showing up. Awareness might be the new bottleneck. It's time to collaborate with Marketing on visibility.

2. **Signups are healthy but activation remains flat:** You improved tutorials and documentation, but developers still aren't reaching "first success." The friction might be in the product, not the learning experience. Or maybe your content isn't reaching them at the right time or place.

3. **Activation improves but retention doesn't:** Developers complete onboarding but don't return. You solved early friction but not long-term engagement. You may need to create advanced examples, deepen community interaction, or highlight features that make the product indispensable.

4. **Retention improves but ARR doesn't:** Developers are active, but they're not converting to paid users. You may be attracting hobbyists or non-commercial users. It might be time to refine your targeting or work more closely with Sales to guide enterprise adoption.

5. **Support ticket volume remains high despite better docs:** Your documentation may have improved in content but not in structure. If discoverability is poor or search is weak, users won't find the answers they need. You may need to rework the information architecture or navigation flow.

Table 6-1 lists some common developer advocacy activities and success metrics that could apply to them.

Table 6-1. *Common developer advocacy activities and their success metrics*

Activity	Success Metrics
Blogs	— Call-to-Action (CTA) Conversion Rate — Pages Per Session — Inbound Links/Backlinks — Scroll Depth — Social Shares and Engagement
Webinars/Hackathons	— No. of Registrations — No. of Attendees — Repo Forks/Code Usage — Question-to-Attendee Ratio — Developer Qualified Leads

(continued)

Table 6-1. *(continued)*

Activity	Success Metrics
Documentation	— Time to First Success — Search-to-No-Ticket Ratio — Internal Search Success Rate — "Edit/Suggest" Click-Throughs — Satisfaction/Sentiment
Libraries/SDK	— Repo Forks/Code Usage — Likes or Stars — API Call Volume
Ambassador Programs	— Quality Contribution Volume — Geographic/Language Reach — Ambassador Retention Rate — Community Deflection Rate (Ambassador-Driven)
Podcasts	— Traffic/Views — Listener-to-Conversion Rate — Completion Rate (per episode)
Videos	— Traffic — Average Video Percentage Viewed — Call-to-Action (CTA) Conversion Rate — Relative Audience Retention
Newsletter	— Subscriber Growth — Open Rate — Click-Through Rate — List Churn Rate — CTA Conversion Rate

(continued)

Table 6-1. *(continued)*

Activity	Success Metrics
Social Media	— Engagement or Replies
	— Community Join Rate
	— Traffic/Likes/Shares/Views
	— CTA Conversion Rate
Training or Certification Programs	— Exam Pass Rate
	— Student Satisfaction Score
	— Completion Rate
Event Sponsorships	— DevRel Qualified Leads
	— Feedback Volume
	— Competitive Intelligence Gained
	— Follow-Up Engagement Rate

The appendix contains definitions for each metric, detailing what they measure and their strategic purpose.

6.3 Identify Your Assist Impact

Developer Relations is in a unique position to do work that supports so many other departments. And when you're reporting your impact, it's important to highlight these assists to show how deeply valuable your work is to the entire organization and further solidify DevRel's place as a strategic function.

While your primary and success metrics measure direct results, **assist metrics** capture DevRel's ripple effects. They prove that your efforts strengthen other functions and make the company more efficient, informed, and customer-centric.

6.3.1 Examples of DevRel Assists

Product: Feedback and Beta Testing

If you're getting exceptional feedback from an individual, passing them directly to Product might be a good idea. The Product team can have a longer conversation with that community member and parse the most valuable insights for future releases.

Likewise, if a group of developers has been asking for a particular feature, you can invite them to test it before public launch. That tight feedback loop improves release quality and builds trust.

Possible metric: Number of community-sourced insights implemented or beta testers recruited.

Engineering: Hard-to-Solve Bugs

At times, you'll meet community members who stumble on particularly difficult bugs and are willing to help your engineering team diagnose them. Making that connection helps both sides; the developer gets a fix, and your engineers save time resolving issues faster.

Possible metric: Number of bugs identified or resolved through community collaboration.

Business Development/Partnerships: Integrations

You might meet developers at other companies who are open to building integrations that help customers use your product alongside theirs. Handing those opportunities to your Partnerships or Business Development team can spark co-marketing efforts and expand your product's reach.

Possible metric: Number of third-party integrations or co-marketing opportunities initiated through DevRel relationships.

Recruiting: Potential New Hires

Occasionally, you'll come across a community member who just *gets it.*
They understand your product deeply, share your mission, and already
contribute to your ecosystem. When a role opens up, they can be an ideal
candidate to pass along to Recruiting.

Possible metric: Number of hires or referrals originating from the
community.

Customer Success: Reduced Support Friction

When DevRel converts repetitive "how-to" questions into documentation
or forum answers, you help reduce the workload on customer support.
That efficiency not only saves time but also improves the developer
experience.

Possible metric: Reduction in repeated support tickets or increase in
self-serve resolution rate.

Marketing and Sales: Leads Handed Off

Developer Relations often sits upstream of meaningful sales conversations,
even if it never closes a deal directly. The relationships you build with
developers in the community can later translate into real pipeline
opportunities when those developers join companies that are evaluating
your product or advocating for it internally.

A developer who has attended your workshops, engaged deeply in
your community, contributed to your open-source projects, or repeatedly
sought guidance may later surface as a strong internal champion inside
a buying organization. Passing that context to Sales gives them a warmer
entry point, shortens discovery, and increases trust early in the cycle.

Possible assist metrics include

- Number of DevRel-sourced leads handed off to Sales or Marketing

- Number of community-sourced customers featured in case studies or references

DevRel assists are a form of organizational leverage. They show that while you may not own a metric like ARR or churn directly, your work accelerates the teams that do.

When you report assists, tie them to tangible downstream outcomes:

- A community-sourced feature improves retention.

- A partnership-driven integration expands product usage.

- A documentation improvement reduces support costs.

- A DQL shortens the sales cycle.

Together, these metrics show that Developer Relations amplifies the impact of every team it touches.

6.4 Calculating ROI of Developer Advocacy

There will come a time when you need to ask for more budget, resources, or even your own promotion. When that time comes, one of the most powerful tools you can have in your arsenal is the ability to quantify the impact of Developer Advocacy in a language executives love: money.

To do that, we can borrow a few lessons from the content marketing world. While Developer Relations isn't content marketing, there are useful parallels we can draw.

6.4.1 Lessons from Zapier: Calculating "Return on DevRel Spend"

Once upon a time, Lane Scott Jones, former Head of Content at Zapier, needed to secure more budget and get her team a seat at the strategy table. But there was one problem. Her boss, the CMO, didn't fully believe in the business impact of content. Coming from a performance marketing background, he was used to clear financial metrics like **Return on Ad Spend (ROAS)**.

So, she decided to speak his language.

Her team created their own version of ROAS: **Return on Content Spend (ROCS)**, shown in Figure 6-2.

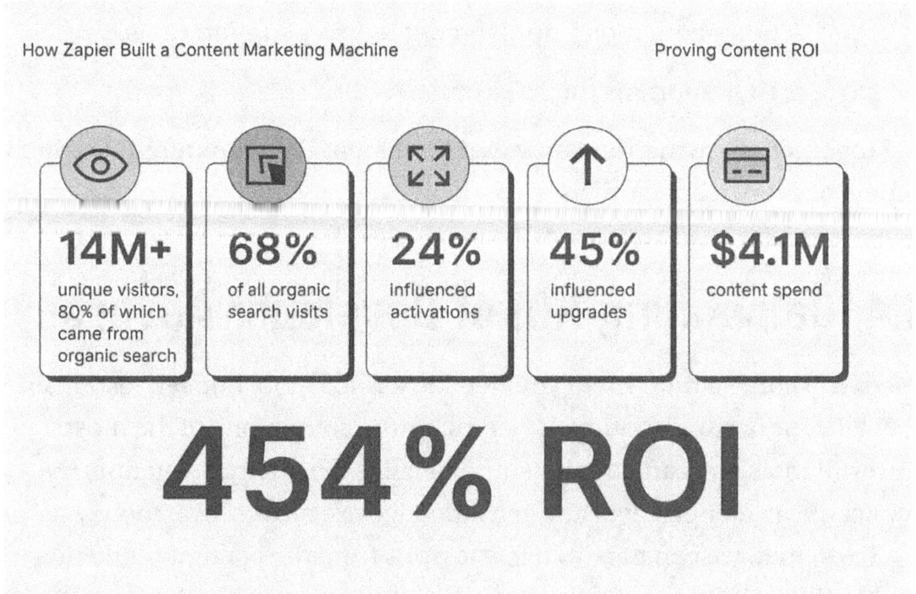

Figure 6-2. *A screenshot from Lane Scott Jones's presentation on her team's ROCS*

Lane Scott Jones and her team tracked all revenue influenced by content signups, then multiplied it by Zapier's average customer lifetime value (LTV)—roughly three years—to estimate long-term revenue impact.

LTV (Lifetime Value) represents how much revenue a customer generates during their relationship with the company. It was included in Zapier's calculation because many of their users paid on a recurring subscription model. Measuring only the first month or year would underestimate the real return.

With an annual content budget of around $1 million (covering salaries, software, data tools, freelancers, and agencies), the team found that content brought in about **$4.1 million in attributed revenue**, resulting in a **454% ROI**.

Now, DevRel isn't content marketing, but you can apply the same principle. The idea is to trace DevRel-attributed actions to measurable business outcomes.

For a self-serve SaaS company, where most developers discover and adopt the product independently, you can

- Track signups originating from DevRel-owned content or campaigns (via UTM links or referral codes). Include DevRel Qualified Leads.

- Calculate revenue from upgrades or feature usage tied to those signups.

- Apply your company's LTV multiplier (e.g., 3 years, like Zapier did) to estimate long-term revenue.

That gives you a simple but powerful formula:

ROI = (Total DevRel-Attributed Revenue ÷ DevRel Spend) × 100

For instance, if your DevRel program costs $500,000 annually and the developers you influence generate $1.5 million in LTV-adjusted revenue, your ROI is 300%.

Having this kind of data is not only persuasive in executive meetings, it's also motivating for your team. It gives everyone a clear, quantifiable sense of how their work drives the company forward.

6.4.2 Beyond Revenue: Quantifying DevRel Influenced Cost Savings

Beyond income generating, Developer Relations also delivers value by reducing costs across other departments. Consider the following categories:

Support cost savings

If community-led support or documentation improvements reduce repetitive "how do I..." tickets by 20%, support engineers can focus more on complex issues, enterprise customers, or proactive improvements. This shift not only improves customer experience but also reduces burnout for the team.

You can put a dollar figure on that impact. Each support ticket carries a cost—time spent by an engineer (typically 15–30 minutes at $30–$50 per hour) plus overhead like tools and management. A conservative estimate is $15–$25 per ticket.

If your community or documentation reduces 3,000 tickets per quarter at $15 each, that translates to $45,000 saved every quarter.

Customer acquisition Cost (CAC) Savings

CAC is the total cost to acquire one new customer. It includes ad spend, events, salaries, tools, and agency fees. When DevRel content, tutorials, or workshops drive organic signups and awareness, they reduce dependency on paid channels.

If marketing spends $200 per paid signup, and DevRel channels generate 1,000 signups organically, that could translate to $200,000 in saved acquisition costs. But before you celebrate, remember to account for the full cost of running the DevRel program—salaries, events, content production, and tools can add up, and the real impact is the savings minus those expenses. For example, if your DevRel program costs $150,000 to run for that period, the net savings is $50,000.

That's why keeping DevRel costs under control is so important. Without careful management, the program can shift from being a source of savings to a high-cost center, which is why it often becomes one of the first teams targeted during budget cuts.

Retention and Churn Reduction

DevRel often improves retention by helping users find value faster, learn more efficiently, and stay engaged.

If developers who attend your workshops have a 10% higher retention rate, and each retained customer adds $500 in annual revenue, that's a measurable gain. Multiply that by your active user base, and the impact compounds over time.

6.4.3 Bringing It All Together

When you combine the elements of revenue generated, costs saved, and retention gains, you can paint a full picture of DevRel's monetary value.

$$\textbf{\textit{DevRel ROI = ((Revenue Generated + Costs Saved)} \div \textbf{\textit{DevRel Spend) x 100\%}}}$$

It's not a perfect science, and it doesn't need to be. What matters is demonstrating that Developer Advocacy drives measurable business outcomes when you need to.

6.5 Communicating Your Developer Advocacy Impact to C-Suite

After you've collated your metric data from whatever source you use, it's time to tell the story that connects the data to the business's journey and its impact.

As an IC in a team, you won't need to bother yourself with this heavy executive reporting. But seeing as this book is for developer advocates who want to start and scale their careers, this is a critical piece to be aware of. When you're promoted to Manager or Head of Department, presenting metrics and communicating the value of your team becomes your core responsibility.

Even before that point, learning to communicate impact is the skill that accelerates your career fastest. When you can connect your daily work to the outcomes that matter to the business, you begin to speak the language of leadership. That shift from "I updated the documentation" to "our documentation updates reduced time-to-first-success by 20%, influencing $X in LTV" is what earns you trust, promotions, and additional resources when/should you ask for it.

For presenting to C-suite, here are some tips I'd recommend:

6.5.1 Match Your Metrics to the Reporting Period

Depending on your company, there will be two main types of reporting periods.

You will usually have **company-wide or business unit-wide high-stakes reports**, often tied to financial quarters or strategic reviews, which happen quarterly or bi-annually. These are the meetings where department heads present to executives and justify past spend or future budgets. In such meetings, executives want answers to one key question: *"What business value did your team deliver this quarter?"* The focus at this level should be on ROI, revenue influenced, costs saved, and the primary metrics that prove the existence and value of your program. For example, you might show how DevRel-led initiatives contributed $300,000 in influenced revenue, reduced support load by 20%, or improved developer onboarding time by 30%.

Then there are **high-cadence reports**, which happen monthly or weekly, such as during internal syncs, all-hands meetings, or department check-ins. These focus on *momentum and learnings* rather than ROI. The question here is, *"What is your team working on right now, and what are you learning?"* For instance, you might report a steady increase in community engagement, early traction for a new tutorial series, or improvements in documentation discoverability that hint at better retention down the line.

6.5.2 Keep Things Short and Sweet

No matter the reporting cadence, your report should be concise, ideally no more than five slides unless otherwise requested. Executives will hear from multiple teams, so your time to capture attention is short.

An executive audience (e.g., CEOs, CMOs, CPOs, or CFOs) does not care about every metric or method. They speak the language of investment, action, and return. They want the big picture: how your work aligns with company goals and what tangible benefits it produces. Focus on outcomes that demonstrate revenue impact, efficiency gains, or other critical business results.

6.5.3 Don't Bury the Lede: Start with the Impact

C-suite attention is brief and measured in money. Start with the results, not the activities.

The first slide of your presentation should be dedicated to presenting the calculated ROI just like the Zapier example, before moving to the how.

For example, going back to the scenarios we introduced in Chapter 4.

The primary goal for the year is to increase user base by 30%, and achieve a 20% increase in annual recurring revenue. And we agreed that our primary DevRel metric will be *"Number of signups or registrations originating from DevRel-owned channels and content."*

Here you want to start with the big picture that shows how your actions have influenced this goal, so you might start with

> "This quarter, DevRel initiatives resulted in 4M unique visitors, of which 20% signed up to try our product, which resulted in $300k of influenced revenue. Our activities also saved the company $50k through support cost savings and churn reduction. Considering that the total DevRel spend for this quarter was $150K, that means that we have a 233% ROI" (Remember our ROI formula).

6.5.4 Use the Body of the Report to Show Causation

Once you have established the headline, you can move into the "how." Summarize the activities that produced these results, perhaps blog articles, videos, starter repos, or product feedback sessions, and show which metrics best reflect their success. You do not need twenty charts; five well-chosen metrics are enough to illustrate your point. These might include

- Growth in newsletter subscribers or YouTube views and subscribers

- Reduction in repetitive support tickets

- Improvement in time to first success

- Number of actionable bugs or insights surfaced from the community

So you might say something like

And we achieved these results with the things we
did this quarter. DevRel produced 10 blog articles,
7 youtube videos, 15 new pieces of documentation,
and conducted a feature review survey within the
community which garnered over 1500 responses.
These activities led to x% increase in newsletter
subscribers or YouTube views, 40% repetition
in support tickets on the xyz issue, and 3 feature
insights which have gone into the product roadmap.
These are the activities that led to the influenced
revenue and support cost savings.

This is a best-case scenario though. It is also likely that your activities
did not yield positive returns and that's when the concluding part of your
presentation comes in handy.

6.5.5 Conclude with Learnings, Next Steps, and an Ask

Your report should close with a forward-looking section. Use data to
reveal bottlenecks, validate assumptions, and justify your next move. Did
your strategic bets hold up? Did a campaign outperform or underperform
expectations? What will you adjust next quarter?

For example:

- **If successful:** "Our new YouTube series doubled the
  video-to-activation rate compared to our team average.
  We'll now hand marketing the assets to scale this
  success through paid promotion."

- **If facing a bottleneck:** "Signups are healthy, but doc
  search success is low. The issue is discoverability. Our
  next step is to rework the information architecture to
  remove friction and shorten time to success."

Summary

Good metrics help you learn what works, improve what doesn't, and communicate your value in a way that business leaders understand. They turn your work from activity into impact. Whether you are tracking time-to-first-success, developer retention, or community engagement, your goal is to connect every data point to the story of how developers succeed because of your efforts.

Metrics are not the enemy of authenticity; they are the bridge between creativity and credibility. Measuring developer advocacy does not cheapen the work; it gives it language and longevity. When you define clear goals, avoid vanity metrics, and align your measurements with company outcomes, you build trust with both your community and your leadership.

At the end of the day, measurement is not just about proving worth. It's about earning the right to keep doing meaningful work, at greater scale, and with greater confidence. So, run toward metrics.

PART III

Advocating for Developers

Up to this point, we have looked at developer advocacy from the inside out: defining the role, building strategy, setting objectives, and aligning with the company's goals. But advocacy is not a one-way broadcast. It is a two-way street. You advocate *to* developers, helping them discover your product, and you advocate *for* developers, bringing their needs and insights back into the company.

This part of the book is about that outward-facing work. Communities (spaces where developers gather, learn, and share) are not just audiences or distribution channels. They are living ecosystems where trust, knowledge, and credibility circulate. Done well, they provide developers with support and belonging, while giving companies a direct line to feedback, champions, and ideas that shape the future of the product.

Some developer advocacy roles are content-centric, while others are community-centric. So far, we've focused on content. **Chapter 7** will explore how to build and nurture these communities, how to establish feedback loops that make developers feel heard, and how to create an environment where your advocacy efforts grow stronger through every interaction.

Building and Nurturing Developer Communities

Building developer communities sounds simple in theory. In practice, it is messy, slow, and often very confusing. And very few people know how to do community better than Ruth Ikegah.

Ruth Ikegah is one person who knows a lot about building, scaling, and nurturing developer communities. She is an Open Source Program Manager, Technical Writer, GitHub Star, and Public Speaker. Ruth leads CHAOSS Africa, where she focuses on improving the health of open source communities across the continent, and she also serves as a maintainer in the project's Diversity, Equity, and Inclusion working group. She has designed programs that span dozens of countries and knows firsthand both the opportunities and the pitfalls of growing communities at scale.

There was nobody better to ask to contribute to this chapter than her.

7.1 What Is a Community?

A community, at its simplest definition, is a group of people who share a common interest. But in practice, communities exist in stages.

© Linda Ikechukwu 2026

L. Ikechukwu, *A Friendly Guide to Developer Advocacy*, Friendly Guides to Technology, https://doi.org/10.1007/979-8-8688-2462-3_7

You might hear a company boast that it has 500,000 community members, only to discover on closer inspection that this means 500,000 emails on a mailing list or maybe that number represents their total number of followings across all social outlets. Fewer than half of that number may have ever signed up for the product, and perhaps only 10% are active users. In that case, can you truly say you have a community of 500,000?

What a community means or who your community is can often be confusing, but it helps to think of community in layers.

7.1.1 The Community at Large

According to SlashData's 2025 *Global Developer Population Trends* report, there are over 47 million developers worldwide.

If you have a developer-facing product, these developers, along with adjacent roles, like solution architects, form your "community at large." They may not know you yet, but they represent the total pool of people who could one day discover and use your product. Your awareness efforts—content, talks, and outreach—are aimed at this group.

7.1.2 Passive Contributors

Once discovered, some people will take small steps to connect with you. They might follow you on social media, sign up for your newsletter, or occasionally lurk in your Slack or forum. They rarely engage publicly, but they still learn from your content and absorb information from others. This group maps to the *Evaluate* and *Learn* stages of the developer journey. In sales terms, they might be considered prospects or leads.

7.1.3 Active Contributors

A smaller group goes further, participating regularly and visibly. They answer questions in your channels, attend webinars, give feedback, or even contribute code or ideas. They may volunteer for beta programs or actively test features. These are active community members. It is important to note that *active product users* are not always the same as *active community members*. Someone might use your product daily and never participate in community activities.

7.1.4 In-Betweeners

Between passive and active contributors, there are those who drift back and forth. Sometimes they are engaged and vocal, and other times they are silent. They may contribute once and then disappear, or spike in activity around a specific project and then go quiet. Depending on your community's size, this can be a wide and elusive group.

7.1.5 The Inner Circle

At the center lies your inner circle. These are active product users who have reached a high level of skill and are also deeply engaged in community life. They are the ones who consistently contribute, provide feedback, and advocate on your behalf. They are your most valuable community members—not because of their number but because of the influence, trust, and continuity they bring to the ecosystem.

7.2 The Value of Community for Companies

Developer advocates who engage with communities benefit greatly, even though it may not be part of their work specification. Communities are vital to the work of developer advocates because strong communities map directly to the objectives developer relations teams have.

Communities drive acquisition by attracting new users. They improve retention by reducing frustration and creating a sense of belonging. They boost engagement by encouraging peer-to-peer activity. They improve support efficiency by enabling members to answer each other's questions. They generate product ideas and influence the roadmap. And they enhance brand reputation by showing the company as credible, trusted, and collaborative.

For companies building developer products, community is not optional. It is one of the strongest levers for growth, trust, and long-term resilience. A product on its own—even a differentiated one—rarely wins by itself. Most developers today have dozens of options to choose from. What tips the balance is not only the product's quality, but also the ecosystem that surrounds it. Communities provide that ecosystem.

1. **Community facilitates Trust and Adoption.**

    Developers are far more likely to adopt a tool when they see people like themselves using it, sharing best practices, and solving problems together. When a developer encounters your product for the first time, they may be skeptical of marketing claims. But when they find a vibrant community where others are openly sharing experiences, solutions, and even code, it builds confidence that your product is worth the investment of their time and attention.

    A thriving community around a service signals trust and momentum. It reassures them that they are not building alone, that others have solved the problems they will encounter, and that help is never far away.

2. **Community facilitates Feedback Loops and Product Evolution.**

One of the most valuable functions of a developer community is the feedback it generates. Communities create a constant stream of insights about how developers are using your product, where they get stuck, and what they wish existed. This feedback is vital because products do not evolve in a vacuum. Some of the most innovative features emerge not from internal roadmaps but from creative ways developers push the product beyond its intended use. Feedback comes in many forms. It could be

- **Friction points:** Repeated questions in forums or Slack channels that highlight confusing workflows.

- **Documentation gaps:** Threads where users clarify what the docs should have explained more clearly.

- **Feature requests:** Recurring asks that suggest missing capabilities or emerging needs.

- **Unintended use cases:** Creative ways developers adapt the product to solve problems the company never anticipated.

Of course, not all feedback is equal. Communities can generate noise as well as signals. The skill lies in identifying patterns: if ten developers struggle with the same setup issue, that is a friction point worth prioritizing. If multiple threads highlight missing documentation, that is a signal to invest in docs. Over time, this creates a virtuous cycle: feedback leads to improvements, improvements make the product better, a better product attracts more users, and more users generate more feedback.

The role of the developer advocate here is twofold. First, to listen: to collect, synthesize, and channel community feedback to the right teams internally. Second, to close the loop: to make sure community members see that their input mattered. When a developer raises an issue and later sees it fixed, with release notes or a blog post acknowledging community input, it builds deep trust. It turns passive users into active advocates.

3. **Community facilitates reach and visibility**.

    Word of mouth among developers is one of the most powerful distribution channels in technology. A company blog post may be skimmed, but a developer recommending your tool in a forum or Slack channel carries real weight. Communities amplify awareness in ways that no single marketing team could replicate.

7.3 If I Had to Build a Community from Scratch

When you join a company without an existing community, the burden might fall on you to build or contribute to building a community.

Communities are built around shared value, so if you cannot yet answer, *"Who should care about this product, and why?" What pain points does your tool relieve? What possibilities does it unlock?*, then you are not ready to invite others in.

Here's how I'd proceed:

7.3.1 Start with the Willing

Your first members are often closer than you think. The first potential members are the people who are already showing interest, whether by using your product, asking questions, or giving feedback.

Your role is to recognize them, bring them together, and create ways for them to contribute. By doing that, you turn scattered signals of interest into the beginnings of an organized, visible community. Their activity then signals to others that your product is worth paying attention to, creating a snowball effect.

7.3.2 Expand to the Broader Ecosystem

Once you've built a space for your existing users, the next step is to expand your efforts into broader communities that intersect with your product. These might be interest-based groups where developers gather around themes like APIs, machine learning, front-end frameworks, databases, or DevOps practices. Or they might be product-based communities centered on tools your product integrates with or builds upon. For example, if your tool extends MongoDB, then MongoDB's community is a natural place to participate.

This expansion matters because developers do not live in a single community. Some may never join your Slack or Discord but they might be deeply engaged on Stack Overflow, Reddit, or independent open-source forums. These spaces are still part of your ecosystem. You cannot control them, but you can contribute authentically by answering questions, sharing resources, and supporting contributors without turning the space into a marketing channel. Done well, this builds a level of awareness, reach, and credibility you cannot achieve through owned channels alone.

The key is to join as a participant rather than a promoter. Learn the culture of the community. Share your journey, ask questions, and add insights unrelated to your product. Over time, you can introduce your company's perspective naturally, and those who find it useful will follow you back into your own space. Developers recognize authenticity instantly, so the value you add to conversations matters more than the frequency of your mentions.

Outreach content can strengthen this presence. Tutorials, blog posts, demos, or videos that solve real problems in the language of the community make your product relevant without being intrusive. For example, if you join an API-focused group and your product simplifies authentication, you might publish a guide on common pitfalls in API authentication, with your tool woven in as part of the solution.

Searching hashtags, digging into subreddit threads, or joining Twitter and LinkedIn groups can reveal these thriving ecosystems where developers already gather.

7.3.3 Nurture Through Authentic Engagement

When you start a community, it will often feel quiet. People join, look around, and say very little. That is normal. Participation grows when you make it safe and worthwhile to speak up. And, the quickest way to get momentum is to engage with intention, and to design the engagement around what members actually value.

Do not assume you know what your community needs or what will work for them. Make discovery a habit. You can use polls in-channel to discover low-friction input on topics, meeting times, and content formats or quick pulse checks to discover what people would like more of or discontinue. Run a two-question form at the end of each month: "What was most useful?" and "What would you like next?" Keep it lightweight so people actually respond.

There are a few engagement strategies you can adopt or even combine for maximum value.

Meetings

Meetings are a simple but powerful way to spark engagement. They give you a chance to connect with real people behind the usernames and start building trust. Done well, they help you learn who your members are, how they use the product, and what challenges they face. These meetings can take different forms that can span the entire month, so you always have regular contact with your community members. These can take several forms:

- **Early adopter or builder calls**: Small-group calls with early users, a monthly "builder's call," or open office hours make members feel like insiders with direct access to your team. For example, an API company might run a monthly feedback session where developers share integration hurdles in real time while the product team listens in. These conversations not only surface insights but also show that member voices matter.

- **Ask Me Anything (AMA) sessions**: Host monthly AMAs with engineers or product leaders who can share insider knowledge that no blog post can replicate. To make them effective, seed five to seven questions in advance and moderate the call so discussions stay focused and engineers can return to their work on time.

- **Feedback or user calls**: If your company ships updates monthly, hold small-group sessions focused on a specific feature, workflow, or pain point. If your release cadence is slower, run these sessions as needed when new features launch. Close the loop by publishing a short findings document in the community and linking to any tickets or PRs created. Always acknowledge contributors by name unless they request otherwise.

- **Community check-ins/office hours**: Schedule a recurring 30–45 minute call where members can drop in, ask questions, or just connect with you and each other. Share product updates, highlight community projects, and answer questions. When possible, vary the meeting time to cover different time zones. When that is not possible, rotate content and always share recaps so everyone benefits.

Content As the Second Touchpoint

Most members will not attend meetings. Content can be the second lane of engagement that mirrors and multiplies your live efforts. It can be in the form of any of the following:

- **Meeting recaps:** Summaries of key discussions from meetings, shared back into the community via newsletters or posts. You can turn the best answers into a FAQ entry or a short blog post so value persists after the live session. This makes members feel included even if they missed the call.

- **Newsletters:** Weekly or monthly digest that includes product updates, "tip of the month," community wins, upcoming calls, and open calls for feedback. This creates a loop that reminds your inactive community members to go check your platform.

- **Tutorials:** Practical resources that help people succeed with the product, often sparked by questions raised in the community itself.

- **Tangential discussions:** Not every post has to be about the product. Allowing discussions on adjacent topics—tools, workflows, or industry news—keeps the space vibrant and broadens participation. This keeps the space useful even when people are not actively debugging your product.

Feedback Loops

Communities grow stronger when members see that their input matters. If someone raises a friction point, acknowledge it, share what action is being taken, and close the loop when it is resolved. When community feedback leads to action, make that visible. Release notes, changelogs, or a post that says, "We fixed this issue thanks to input from our community" builds enormous goodwill. Developers who see their feedback acted on often become long-term advocates.

Recognition and Incentives

Nothing deepens loyalty like being recognized. You can weave in recognition into your operations without it costing so much in dime and time. You can start with:

- **Public acknowledgment:** A weekly or monthly shout-out in a newsletter, a thank-you tweet, or a "Member Spotlight" post in your forum for members who made useful contributions like clever use cases, a published tutorial using your product, answering questions, open source contributions, feedback, or something for that month.

- **Swag and merchandise:** Every month, you can send out stickers, shirts, or mugs or other small but tangible tokens of appreciation to your recognized members.

- **Product incentives:** For members who you cannot ship stuff out to perhaps for distance or whatever reason, you can offer credits, free or upgraded access, or invitations to test unreleased features that signal that the company values their contributions.

Nudges

At the start of a community, every relationship matters, and anything you can do to encourage more participation should be explored. Recognition will keep your most active members motivated, but nurturing a community also means encouraging participation from those who are less vocal. Not everyone will jump in on their own, and that's where nudges come in.

I found this simple low-tech method shared by Noele Flowers for nudging your less-participatory community members to become more active.

At the start of each month, select about 20 community members outside of your champions and group them into two categories:

- ◍ **Yellow :**These members only engage occasionally, usually when tagged or prompted. Your goal here is habit-building. Involve them directly: tag them in questions you know they can answer, invite them to host a small ritual like a "tip of the week," or ask them to share their workflow.

- ● **Red:** These are members who have joined but remain silent. Your goal is activation. A personal nudge can go a long way: reach out with a direct message, invite them for a quick coffee chat, or ask a simple, low-barrier question that gets them to speak up for the first time.

At the end of the month, reassess where each person stands. Some will move up, others will remain where they are, and that is fine.

Healthy communities always have a mix of highly active, moderately active, and silent members. What matters is that you create clear pathways for those who *do* want to deepen their engagement. Of course this method does not need to scale but it helps to build close relationships with your early community members.

7.3.4 Scale with Programs

Once your community has settled into steady engagement, and you have more resources and budget, you can begin to scale by creating focused programs that extend your reach and growth beyond what you and your team alone can manage.

There are a couple of ways to do this:

Ambassador Programs

As your community matures, one of the most powerful ways to scale is through ambassadors. Ambassadors take your story into places, regions, countries, ecosystems, and networks you could never reach on your own, and they do it with a level of authenticity no marketing campaign can buy.

For example, once upon a time, Ruth was contacted to help expand a GitHub curriculum/course on open source contribution (initially run in the United States) into the African tech ecosystem. She designed an ambassador program with leaders in West, East, South, North, and Central Africa. Each ambassador leveraged their own networks and influence, which is how the program quickly spread into 27 countries.

Many successful companies have shown what using ambassador programs to scale can look like; from programs like GitHub Stars, Cloud Native Ambassadors, GitHub Student Experts, Microsoft MVP, and so on.

Geshan Manandhar maintains a GitHub repo list of developer programs run by different companies so you can draw inspiration from here: `https://github.com/geshan/developer-ambassador-programs`

Finding ambassadors begins with noticing who is already visible. They are the people who stand out in your ecosystem, the bloggers who share tutorials about your product, the engineers who take the initiative to build tools or open-source extensions, the active participants in your forums or social channels, the vocal champions.

These individuals have already signaled their commitment and energy. You just need to recognize that energy and give it structure. At some point, recognition alone won't cut it. The most effective companies formalize ambassadorship into programs people aspire to. GitHub Stars, Cloud Native Ambassadors, GitHub Student Experts, and Microsoft MVPs, all of these have built-in prestige. People brag about them, add them to résumés, and work hard to stay active enough to keep the title.

Your program needs to be both aspirational and accountable. Give it a clear identity and transparent guiding principles. Limit the term length so that ambassadors must remain active to retain their title. Define the nomination and renewal process openly, so members see it as fair. And make the benefits meaningful enough to motivate, such as

- Recognition and personal branding opportunities

- Early or exclusive access to features

- Invitations to company or developer events

- Travel or accommodation support for speaking engagements

- Product credits or free access

- Budget to host local learning events around your product

For a more tactical starting point, Jan Schenk has even published a sample ambassador program draft that you can adapt as inspiration when structuring your own DevRel programs: `https://github.com/jansche/oss-advisors`

Hackathons

Hackathons and builder challenges are another way to scale your community once the basics are in place. Unlike meetups or AMAs, hackathons give you not only the chance to put your product in people's hands but they also expose, in a compressed time frame, exactly what delights them and what gets in their way.

When done well, hackathons can be one of the most effective tools in your DevRel playbook, delivering ROI in ways few other activities can.

- **Acquisition and Activation:** Nothing drives first runs of your product like a hackathon. With hands-on time, mentors on site, and teammates cheering each other on, developers get past setup friction and actually build something. Twilio famously used hackathons in its early days to get developers, sending their first SMS in minutes, which later translated into long-term product adoption.

- **Feedback Loops:** Hackathons compress weeks of product usage into hours. The friction points that normally take months to emerge in production show up within hours, because hackathon participants hit every edge case at speed. If your onboarding is broken, you will know by lunchtime. If your docs are unclear, you'll get the same question 20 times in a row. That kind of feedback is gold for a DevRel team. IBM's evangelists used to leave hackathons with detailed debriefs highlighting where new developers struggled, which directly informed doc updates and product fixes.

- **Content Pipeline:** A good hackathon doesn't end at the closing demos. Follow up immediately. Collect repos, screenshots, and quotes, then turn the most interesting projects into blog posts, tutorials, or showcase pages. Every hackathon should leave you with a content pipeline of multiple "how they built it" writeups, sample code pulled from winning teams, or new recipes that demonstrate your API in action. At the same time, you need to close the loop internally. Log the friction you saw. Update the docs or SDKs. File issues or PRs where appropriate. Share a crisp debrief with engineering, product, and leadership so the lessons don't evaporate when the event ends.

- **R&D and New Ideas:** Hackathons are a low-risk lab for generating real business options. Give developers a broad challenge, and they'll push your product into directions you never considered— extensions, integrations, or entirely new use cases. At a Wimbledon-themed hackathon, teams came up with ideas to improve fan experience during matches, from real-time seat upgrades to data-driven concessions. None of these ideas were on the host company's roadmap, but some became viable pilots. For your product, a hackathon prototype might reveal a new market segment, a missing feature that unlocks adoption, or even a whole product line you could consider.

- **Internal Trust:** In a world of shrinking budgets, hackathons can be defended because they produce tangible outputs: new users onboarded, feedback captured, and content created.

Guest Writing Programs

Another powerful way to scale your community is by inviting members to write with you. Blog posts, tutorials, and case studies don't always need to come from inside your company. In fact, when they come from community members, they often carry more weight. Developers trust peers who are solving real problems far more than polished marketing copy.

The benefits run both ways. For contributors, it's visibility. Seeing their name on a company blog with distribution to thousands of readers is something they can showcase on LinkedIn or add to their résumé.

There's also financial value. Many companies pay anywhere from $100 to $400 per post. For your company, it's authentic content you didn't have to write yourself and new perspectives that reveal use cases your team may never have imagined. You provide the platform, editorial support, and amplification. They provide the story.

Plenty of companies have shown how impactful this can be:

- **Auth0** built an engineering blog where many of the most popular tutorials came from outside contributors.

- **DigitalOcean's Community tutorials** became a go-to developer resource because they paired contributors with editors, building a library of content that still drives massive organic traffic today.

- **HashiCorp** regularly features "how we built it" stories from users, which double as authentic case studies and proof points for the product.

The key to making a guest writing program successful is lowering the barrier to entry. Not every developer is a polished writer, and that's okay. Offer scaffolding: a simple pitch form, outline templates, and light editing to help contributors shine. Recognize their work, promote it widely, and make the experience rewarding.

Done right, a guest writing program strengthens both your content and your community. It sends a clear signal: *this isn't just our platform, it's yours too.*

7.4 If I Had to Steer an Existing Community

Sometimes you inherit an already existing community. In these cases, your first responsibility is not to make sweeping changes, but to build trust.

Trust is fragile when you are new. Members may have seen other leaders or advocates come and go. Show up first as a listener. Spend time observing how the community communicates, what rituals or norms already exist, and who the informal leaders are. Participate in conversations without steering them. Ask questions, thank people for their contributions, and learn the history of how the group came together.

There will be temptation when you inherit a community to fix what looks broken. But respect must come before reform. Even if you have bold new ideas, imposing them too quickly can fracture what trust is already there.

A better approach is gradual evolution. Start by reinforcing what's working. If there's a tradition of weekly demos or open office hours, attend them, amplify them, and celebrate participants. Then, over time, introduce new practices in small, visible steps. This could be in the form of an updated code of conduct, a more streamlined feedback process, or new content formats. Each change should come with context: explain why you're making it, how it aligns with the community's goals, and how you've incorporated feedback.

Above all, continuity matters. Communities thrive when members feel that their contributions are valued and that the space belongs to them, not just the company. By honoring existing patterns and introducing changes slowly, you preserve the community's sense of ownership while still guiding it toward greater impact.

7.5 Measuring Community Health

To keep getting buy-in for community work, you have to show impact. But measuring community health is tricky. The easy numbers—Slack signups, Discord members, Twitter followers—rarely tell the whole story. A community with ten thoughtful contributors can be far healthier than one with ten thousand lurkers. Vanity metrics may look impressive in a slide deck, but they don't tell you if the community is thriving or helping the business.

At the simplest level, a healthy community is one where people participate, return, and contribute in meaningful ways. That might look like consistent conversation in forums, recurring attendance at meetings, or pull requests being merged in an open-source project.

It might also look like developers sharing feedback, answering each other's questions, or advocating for your tool inside their companies. What matters is not just activity, but continuity and impact. Do contributors come back after their first pull request? Do users who join a call or workshop show up again? Are new members joining while others remain engaged? These are the kinds of signals that indicate health and impact.

Because every community is different, you need a framework to avoid chasing noise. One practical approach is the **Goal–Question–Metric (GQM)** framework, illustrated in Table 7-1. Instead of asking "what can we measure?", you start with what matters for the company and work backward.

1. **Set the Goal:** Tie it directly to a company outcome.

2. **Ask the Questions:** What evidence would show that community activity is contributing to this goal?

3. **Pick the Metrics:** The specific things you will track to answer those questions.

For example:

Table 7-1. *Example application of the Goal–Question–Metric (GQM)*
framework to different goal scenarios

Company outcome	Questions	Metrics
Grow adoption in new regions.	— Are we seeing new contributors from outside our core geography? — Are they staying engaged beyond the first interaction?	— Geographic diversity of active members (contributors, forum posts, event attendees). — Return rates (percentage of first-time contributors who come back in the next quarter).
Strengthen retention and reduce churn.	— Do members who engage in community stick with the product longer? — Does community activity reduce support load, improve docs, or feed into product roadmap?	— Comparison of retention rates for active community members vs. silent users. — Percentage of support questions answered by the community instead of staff. — Number of product features borne from community suggestions.

(continued)

Table 7-1. (*continued*)

Company outcome	Questions	Metrics
Build awareness.	– Is the community amplifying our story outside our channels? – Are we creating visible advocates?	– Mentions of the product in independent blogs, talks, or social media. – Number of members producing tutorials, demos, or talks. – Number of weekly new topics in Discourse/StackOverflow/GitHub Discussions – Number of user contributions (whether it is PRs, questions, answers, etc.)

Notice that in each case, the metric is not just "activity for activity's sake" but something that connects community signals to business impact. Focus less on how loud your community is, and more on whether it's helping the company build better products, keep more users, and earn more trust. You also want to track the month-over-month of these metrics so that when there is a rise or fall, you can dig deeper to diagnose why.

Summary

Building and nurturing developer communities is equal parts patience and intention. You start with a few curious users, create space for them to connect, and engage them in ways that make participation feel rewarding. Over time, trust grows, feedback flows, and the community becomes a partner in shaping both product and narrative. Scaling then comes from empowering others—through ambassador programs, guest content, or hackathons—to carry the story into new spaces and networks.

You might find this community launch guide helpful: `https://docs.google.com/document/d/1qEsTpoLZZoygWK66db3o1y9NUcSmgx3_WQUG8fPfHuO/edit?ref=devrelresourc.es&ref=devrelresourc.es&tab=t.0#heading=h.791otcdvwuom`

PART IV

Landing the Developer Advocacy Job

So far, this book has covered the full landscape of developer advocacy. We began with the fundamentals: what the role is, what it entails, and the kind of person who thrives in it. We then turned to strategy, showing how to design and execute impactful programs that serve both developers and the business.

We explored the formats that bring advocacy to life, from talks to blogs to video, and looked at how to measure impact with the right metrics. Finally, we examined advocacy in the other direction: building communities, creating feedback loops, and improving the developer experience itself.

Now the focus shifts to you. How can you take all the knowledge you've learned to land a developer advocacy job and build a career you'll love? The next two chapters are just about that.

CHAPTER 8

Breaking into Developer Advocacy

This chapter discusses how to become a developer advocate. If you are reading this book, you have already taken the first step: educating yourself. What follows is the practical path from an aspiring advocate to a practicing one: how to build a portfolio without formal experience, how to prepare for interviews, and how to recognize red flags when evaluating opportunities.

8.1 Building a Developer Advocacy Portfolio

People arrive at developer advocacy from different paths. Some transition from software engineering, technical writing, community organizers, customer success, and so much more. There is no single background that guarantees success in DevRel. What could improve your odds of getting in though is putting together a portfolio which demonstrates that you already understand what the job entails and have practiced the core skills, whether or not you've held the title before.

There are many ways to start: writing about tools you enjoy, answering questions on Stack Overflow, speaking at a local meetup, contributing documentation to an open source project, or volunteering to improve onboarding materials at your current company.

Here's a systematic approach to putting your portfolio together.

© Linda Ikechukwu 2026
L. Ikechukwu, *A Friendly Guide to Developer Advocacy*, Friendly Guides to Technology,
https://doi.org/10.1007/979-8-8688-2462-3_8

8.1.1 Step 1: Pick a Tool or Product You Love

Choose a product you genuinely enjoy, the one you find yourself reaching for or can't do without. The reason is authentic enthusiasm is hard to fake, and it shows up in your work. If you love the tool, you'll naturally dig deeper, share more, and sustain the effort long enough to produce meaningful work.

It'd also be great if the tool meets a certain level of credibility. If you pick a brand-new library that nobody has heard of, your work may not reach an audience large enough to demonstrate your skills. On the other hand, you don't need to choose React or Kubernetes either. The goal is to find a balance: a product with enough adoption to give your content traction, but not so saturated that your voice gets lost in the noise.

For example, one early-career advocate I coached loved using Supabase for side projects. Instead of chasing the React content wave, she built a series of short tutorials around Supabase authentication. Those tutorials quickly picked up attention on Twitter and Reddit because Supabase was gaining momentum at the time, and her work filled a real need. By the time she interviewed for her first DevRel role, she could point to concrete examples of helping a developer community, and she had evidence of engagement to back it up.

Once you've got a product or tool picked, it's time to pretend that whatever company made that tool or service hired you to do developer relations for them. What would you do? What would be your goal? Remember all we discussed about coming up with a strategy in Chapters 4 and 5.

8.1.2 Step 2: Research the Wins, Friction, and Pain

Once you've picked your product, your next task is to research how developers actually experience it. This is where you step into the advocate's mindset—observing, listening, and surfacing patterns across the whole developer journey, starting from the SDKs, the APIs, the documentation, the signup flow, the buying process, and even the customer service experience. This will go into shaping your strategy.

Start by looking outward:

- GitHub issues often reveal recurring frustrations or missing features.

- Twitter and Reddit threads highlight what excites developers, what confuses them, and what sparks debate.

- Stack Overflow and community forums surface the "how do I…" questions that documentation hasn't yet answered.

- Blog posts and release notes can provide hints of where the product shines and where it has historically stumbled.

Then, balance that with your own experience. Ask yourself:

- Why do I keep reaching for this tool?

- Where does it interrupt my flow?

- What parts would overwhelm a beginner?

- What would make me stop using it altogether?

The goal is to map the product's **wins, friction, and pain points** in a way that feels concrete. Wins show you where to amplify and celebrate. Friction points suggest content opportunities: tutorials, explanations, or examples that smooth the path. Pain points highlight where the product or documentation falls short, which you can later translate into feedback or even portfolio projects like improved docs.

Take Supabase as an example.

- **Wins:** Developers rave about how quickly you can spin up a database and authentication system.

- **Friction:** The docs around custom rules feel thin, leaving gaps that trip people up.

- **Pain:** Reports of scaling issues surface when projects grow beyond a certain size.

8.1.3 Step 3: Use Your Research to Create a Strategy

By now, you should have a clear picture of what delights developers about your chosen tool and where they get stuck. The next step is to turn those insights into a developer relations strategy. In practice, this means mapping your notes on wins, friction, and pain to the four major pillars of DevRel: awareness, education, feedback, and community.

Suppose you chose Supabase. In your research, you might have found that developers love the ease of spinning up a Postgres database, but they often struggle with poorly documented processes for configuring authentication for edge cases like passwordless login or third-party providers. You could turn that friction into a personal DevRel strategy like this:

- **Awareness:** Could you create a conference talk, podcast appearance, or short explainer video that introduces the tool and highlights how it solves that pain? For Supabase, you can write a short post on Twitter or LinkedIn comparing Supabase auth to Firebase, highlighting how simple the Supabase approach is for basic cases. Pair it with a short video snippet to catch attention.

- **Education:** Could you write a tutorial, record a demo, or publish a blog post showing exactly how to work around the friction you found? For example, you can create a tutorial titled *"How to set up passwordless login with Supabase in Next.js"*. Walk through it step by step, using clear code snippets and screenshots.

- **Feedback:** Could you engage the community in a forum thread or GitHub discussion to surface other developers' experiences and share them back with the project maintainers? For example, you can start a GitHub discussion or Reddit thread asking others about their biggest Supabase auth challenges. Summarize the responses and feed them back into your content.

- **Community:** Could you amplify the work of other developers who are already solving this problem, turning their solutions into stories or case studies? For example, you can share projects from developers who have already built creative auth workflows with Supabase. Showcase them in a blog post or video roundup, giving credit while amplifying their work.

You do not need to cover all four pillars right away. What matters is that you show your ability to think like an advocate. You are not just producing content at random, but tying your work to real developer needs and aligning it with broader goals that move the needle.

8.1.4 Step 4: Measure Your Impact and Use Feedback to Improve

Publishing is not the finish line. In Chapter 6, we discussed how to promote and distribute your work so it reaches developers. That still applies here. Go promote it. Give it every chance to be seen.

If you want to take it further, consider publishing beyond your own channels. Many companies run guest author programs, and their blogs often have much larger audiences than yours. They are usually looking for fresh content and sometimes pay for contributions. A quick search can uncover the right contact in content or marketing who might welcome your piece.

The next step is to measure impact and learn from it. To grow as an advocate, you need to measure the impact of what you produce and feed that learning back into your next piece. This is exactly how DevRel operates inside companies, and showing that you can do it on your own will set you apart in interviews.

Start with simple signals. Track how many people read your article, watched your video, or shared your post. Look at comments, retweets, or upvotes to see if your content resonated. Did someone say your guide helped them solve a real problem? Did maintainers acknowledge your contribution or link to your work? These signs often mean more than raw numbers.

Feedback is the other half of the loop. If you see recurring comments pointing out confusion or missing details, take that as a sign to refine your content. For example, if several developers note that your Supabase passwordless login tutorial did not cover third-party providers, you could release a follow-up that fills that gap. Positive feedback is just as important. If developers are sharing your work widely, that tells you you have struck a chord, and you can build on that format or topic.

Imagine walking into an interview and being able to say something like, "Over the last six months, I've been executing a personal developer relations strategy for Supabase. I've created 12 pieces of content which have reached 15k developers. My work has also led to Feature A, Bug Fix B, and Docs Improvement C." No hiring manager will be able to overlook that.

8.1.5 Step 5: Package Your Work into a Portfolio

The final step is to pull everything together into a single, polished portfolio that you can share with hiring managers. This is what elevates you from "someone who has blog posts scattered across the Internet" to "someone with a proven strategy." It then becomes something you link directly on your resume, LinkedIn, or personal site. It gives interviewers a *story* they can follow, instead of a random collection of links.

You do not need a fancy website to start. A Notion page, a Google Doc, Canva sites, or a simple static site will work. The goal is to present your work as a *case study*, showing not just what you created but how you approached it like a developer advocate.

A simple structure could include the following sections, as shown in Figure 8-1:

1. **Title and problem statement**

   Example: *Improving Supabase Authentication Onboarding*

   One or two sentences describing the problem you noticed ("Developers often struggled to configure passwordless login because documentation was incomplete").

2. **Research and insights**

   A brief summary of what you found (wins, frictions, pains). Mention how you listened to the community, read GitHub issues, or followed Twitter/Reddit threads.

3. **Your strategy**

   Outline how you mapped those insights into one or two DevRel pillars (awareness, education, community, feedback). Be concise.

4. **Content created**

   List and link to your outputs: blogs, talks, tutorials, videos. Each with one line explaining the intent.

5. **Impact**

   Highlight key metrics (views, stars, retweets, comments, sign-ups if available). Include qualitative wins like "Maintainer X retweeted this" or "Three developers commented that this tutorial solved their issue."

6. **Takeaways**

   End with a short reflection on what worked and what you would improve if you had more time. This shows maturity and self-awareness.

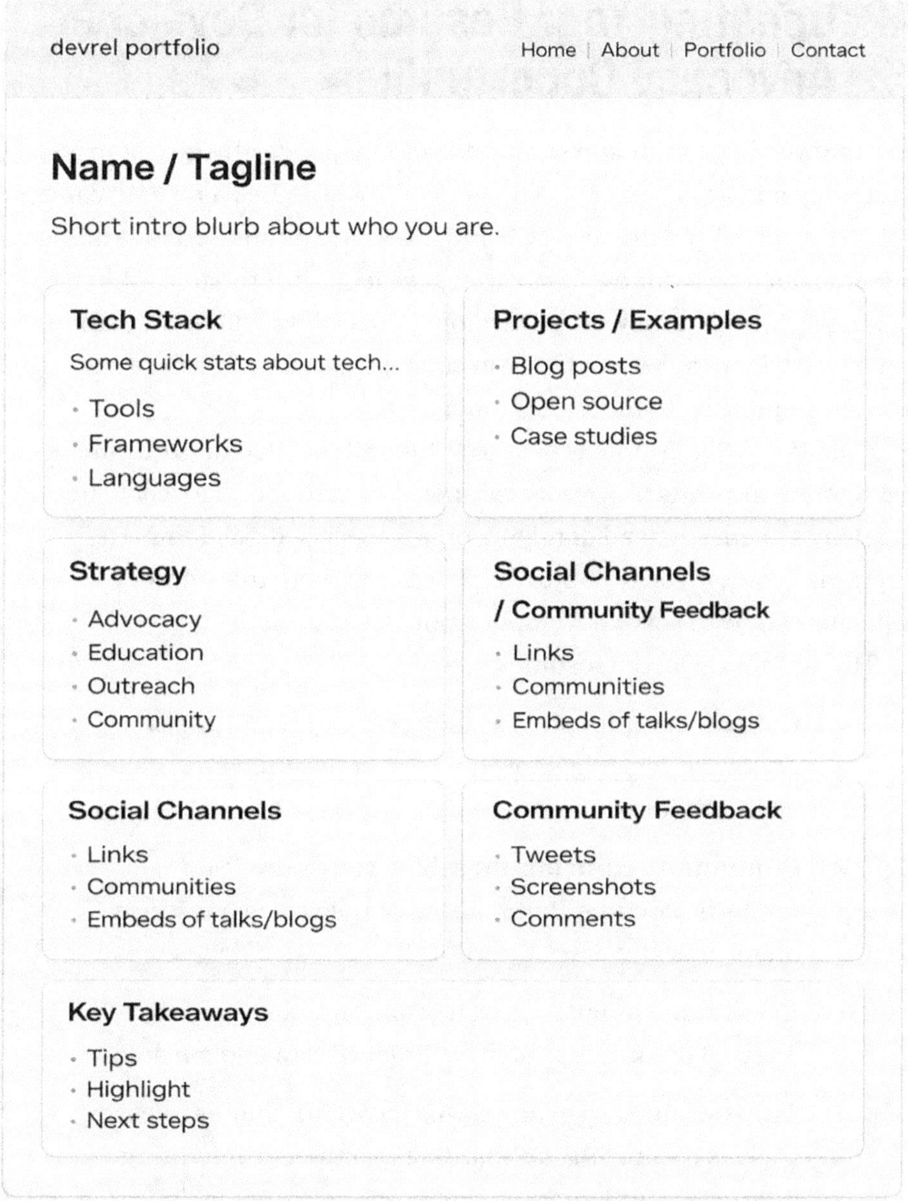

devrel portfolio   Home | About | Portfolio | Contact

Name / Tagline

Short intro blurb about who you are.

Tech Stack

Some quick stats about tech...

- Tools
- Frameworks
- Languages

Projects / Examples

- Blog posts
- Open source
- Case studies

Strategy

- Advocacy
- Education
- Outreach
- Community

Social Channels / Community Feedback

- Links
- Communities
- Embeds of talks/blogs

Social Channels

- Links
- Communities
- Embeds of talks/blogs

Community Feedback

- Tweets
- Screenshots
- Comments

Key Takeaways

- Tips
- Highlight
- Next steps

Figure 8-1. *Developer advocacy portfolio sample*

8.2 Updating Your Resume for Developer Advocacy Opportunities

Now that you have built and packaged your evidence, the next step is presenting it in a way that gets you noticed. For DevRel, a resume cannot look like a generic engineering CV. Engineers are often used to sending the same document for every role, because technical recruiters filter by languages and frameworks. Developer advocacy is different. Hiring managers want to see proof that you can teach, communicate, and represent a product to other developers.

A good DevRel resume is bespoke. Tailor it for each opportunity, highlighting the parts of your experience that map most closely to the company's needs. Instead of relying on a one-size-fits-all template, emphasize your advocacy potential. Lead with work that shows you understand how to serve developers, not just write code.

The strongest DevRel resumes include

- **Content samples** such as blog posts, talks, tutorials, or newsletters that show how you communicate technical ideas.

- **Community contributions** like open-source pull requests, documentation fixes, or answering questions on forums and Stack Overflow.

- **Event experience** such as hackathons, meetups, or internal workshops you have organized or spoken at.

- **Transferable advocacy skills** drawn from other roles, such as mentoring, onboarding teammates, or writing internal documentation, that prove you already do parts of the job.

- **Quantified impact** wherever possible. Instead of writing "spoke at conferences," say "delivered three conference talks reaching 1,200 developers, resulting in 400 GitHub stars on the showcased project." Numbers give hiring managers a clear link between your work and outcomes.

To help, here's a sample resume for a Support Engineer pivoting into Developer Advocacy. Notice how it highlights transferable skills from support, then brings in a structured DevRel portfolio project to fill the experience gap. The format is clean, ATS-friendly, and emphasizes impact with quantified outcomes. Use this as inspiration to shape your own resume, tailored to your background, your projects, and the role you are aiming for, as shown in Figure 8-2.

Find a downloadable copy here: `https://bit.ly/sample-dev-advocate-resume`

Jane Kowalska

Dev Advocate

123 Your Street, Your City, ST 12345

123.456.7890 | no_reply@example.com | github | linkedin |

JavaScript, TypeScript, React, PostgreSQL, Supabase, REST APIs, GitHub, Notion

About

I am a Support Engineer pivoting into Developer Advocacy, with six years of experience helping developers succeed through technical troubleshooting, clear documentation, and community engagement. My work has always gone beyond closing tickets. I write tutorials, improve onboarding flows, and surface developer pain points to product teams.

Experience

Since I do not yet have formal DevRel experience, I challenged myself to design and execute a full strategy for Supabase. I identified developer pain points, created content to address them, and engaged the community for feedback, resulting in blogs, tutorials, and discussions that reached thousands of developers and produced actionable insights for the ecosystem. Packaged the project into a public portfolio site, complete with metrics, qualitative feedback, and reflections *here.*

- Authored tutorials such as *"How to set up passwordless login with Supabase in Next.js"* that generated **5,000+ views** and was referenced in **three GitHub discussions**.
- Created two short explainer videos introducing Supabase authentication, each exceeding **1,200 views in the first week**.
- Initiated and moderated community threads on Reddit and GitHub, collecting **50+ developer insights**, which were summarized and shared with maintainers.
- Curated and amplified community-built Supabase projects, resulting in a **30% increase in engagement** on developer showcases.

Employment History

Support Engineer, XYZ Tech (Remote) - *2018–Present*

- Resolved 1,200+ developer issues annually, maintaining a **95% satisfaction rating**.
- Authored 12 onboarding guides and FAQs later adopted into the official developer portal **reducing new-user support tickets by 20%**.
- Partnered with product teams to prioritize three SDK usability improvements based on developer pain points surfaced through support.

Technical Support Specialist, ABC Systems — *2016–2018*

- Diagnosed and resolved integration issues for **200+ enterprise developers**, ensuring smooth adoption of SaaS APIs.
- Produced internal documentation that cut support resolution time by **18%** and was later published in customer onboarding flows.
- Provided structured product feedback that informed **two new API features** adopted by the engineering team.

Education

AGH University of Science and Technology, Kraków
Bachelor's Degree, Honors. Computer Science and Econometrics — 2016

Figure 8-2. *Sample developer advocacy resume showing how to present transferable skills from previous experience*

Additionally, if you can, I'd also recommend including a cover letter. They are a great opportunity to showcase your writing skills when applying for a DevRel role. You can explain in further detail why you want to be considered for the role, explain your resume a bit more and offer some background about why you are interested in working at the company you're applying to.

8.3 Finding Developer Advocacy Opportunities

Unlike traditional engineering jobs, DevRel openings are not always listed on standard job boards. Many are shared through networks, communities, or even casually on social media. To avoid missing out, you need a strategy that combines public job boards with community-driven channels.

Where to look for DevRel jobs:

- **LinkedIn and personal networking**: Many roles are first posted on LinkedIn. Set up keyword alerts for "Developer Advocate," "Developer Relations," or "DevRel Engineer." Engage with hiring managers and share insights to raise your visibility.

- **Communities**: Join Slack and Discord spaces like the DevRel Collective. Many companies post roles in these channels before announcing them publicly.

- **Conferences and meetups**: Events like DevRelCon, local developer meetups, and hackathons often surface hiring opportunities through informal conversations.

- **Company websites**: If you have a shortlist of dream companies, check their careers pages regularly. Some developer-first organizations only post jobs on their own site.

- **Job boards**: Use sites like Indeed, Otta, <u>startup.jobs</u>, <u>devrelcareers.com</u> , or other developer-focused platforms, filtering for relevant titles.

- **Social media**: Twitter, Reddit, and LinkedIn remain active hubs for job announcements. Following advocates and DevRel leaders often gives you early notice.

- **Recruitment and referrals**: Recruiters sometimes approach directly on LinkedIn. Referrals from current employees remain one of the strongest ways to get noticed.

- **Search engines**: Simple keyword searches like "Developer Advocate jobs" or "DevRel Engineer roles" can uncover listings scattered across smaller boards or company pages.

Another tip that may increase your surface area of luck in attracting opportunities is building in public. Imagine that when Jane Kowalska began her Supabase portfolio challenge, she announced her intent to move into Developer Advocacy and shared updates on Twitter and LinkedIn. She posted progress reports, asked questions, and invited feedback from the community. This will create two benefits: first, it'll give her accountability and encouragement to keep going, and second, it will make her visible to hiring managers who could see her genuine interest and growth.

8.4 Acing Developer Advocacy Interviews

Before even sending in your application for a role, it might be worth taking some time to evaluate if a company and their product are the right fit for you. Not every job is worth applying for if you want to give yourself a better chance at success. P.S., these considerations also apply when you're contemplating on whether to accept an offer.

- **Consider the product and company fit:** Start with the basics: Use the product. Sign up, install the SDK, build a quick demo. Take note of where it shines and where it frustrates you. If you cannot quickly get to a "hello world," or if the product feels broken or misaligned with your interests, that is a signal. Your day-to-day job will be showing this experience to others, so you must genuinely believe in it. Where is the product headed? Do you agree with that vision, and does it align with your own career goals? You are not just taking a job; you are lending your voice, face, and reputation to that company's brand. If you cannot stand behind their trajectory, you will struggle in the role. Be sure to thoroughly read the role requirements, check out the company's website, recent blogs, major announcements, listing on Crunchbase and reviews from Glassdoor. Also make use of your own network and try to find someone who has firsthand experience with the company.

- **Consider company health and structure**: Research the company. Look them up on Crunchbase or Glassdoor to understand their health. Scan LinkedIn for how the DevRel team is structured and whether they have one at all. If you are joining as the first advocate, you will likely need to wear many hats and build programs from scratch. If you are joining an established team, the role may be narrower, but you'll have clearer support and infrastructure. It's great to know what you're signing up for and if you have the capacity to execute. If you're a junior professional, it is especially important to join a team where there is at least one experienced advocate who can mentor you. Without that, you may find yourself trying to invent both the role and the strategy from scratch, which can be overwhelming. You should also find out where DevRel sits in the organization. A team that reports into engineering may push harder on SDKs, APIs, and code contributions. A team under marketing may prioritize content, events, and lead-tracking. Neither is wrong, but you want to pick a role that plays more to your strength. Whether that's the content, code, or community side of things.

- **Consider potential career capital**: Ask yourself: what will I learn here, how useful will it be, and how quickly will I grow? Who will you be working with and meeting? The people around you can shape your trajectory as much as the work itself. Strong peers, thoughtful collaborators, and experienced mentors can accelerate your growth and open new doors. Consider the culture. Will this environment help you grow as a person?

If you've decided that a job is worth applying to, then these are tips that will help you increase your chances for success.

8.4.1 Research the Product (and Company)

Most DevRel roles, including the ones where you will be joining an established DevRel team, require you to be a self-starter with ideas. It's important that before the interview, you research the company you are applying to and come up with some concrete ideas of how you can contribute to their program. Think about two or three specific contributions you could make. That might be running workshops to address a gap you noticed in onboarding, creating a video tutorial around a common GitHub issue, or suggesting a community program that complements their current efforts.

One of the first questions you may hear is, "Have you tried our product?" and the worst possible answer is no. At a minimum, sign up, install the SDK, and build a quick demo. Be ready to share your first impressions, including both what worked and where you struggled.

8.4.2 Demonstrate Core DevRel Traits

DevRel interviews are not only about what you know, but how you work with others. Employers will test whether you have the qualities that make someone effective in the role. Expect scenario-based questions that ask you to draw on past experiences. Preparing examples of when you demonstrated these traits from previous experiences in advance will help you.

- **Empathy:** The most important trait in developer advocacy is empathy. Technical skills can be learned on the job, but empathy has to be present from day one. Advocates need to genuinely care about their users and community. Think about moments when you yourself were stuck for hours on a missing line of documentation. The right response to that pain is not to dismiss it but to say, "That sucks, let's make it better." Companies want to see you demonstrate that instinct, so prepare examples where you helped someone overcome a frustrating technical hurdle.

- **Love of learning:** DevRel demands a constant appetite for learning. Unlike engineering roles where you can settle into familiar codebases, in advocacy you are always experimenting with new tools and then explaining how they fit into real-world use cases. Employers look for signs of curiosity and adaptability. Be ready with a story of when you picked up a new framework, quickly got it working, and then shared what you learned with others.

- **Ability to juggle multiple projects:** Developer advocates rarely focus on just one thing. In a single week, you might be building a demo app, preparing slides for a conference, editing a video tutorial, and reporting on community metrics. The ability to manage several different projects at once, often across unrelated skill domains, is a core part of the job. Prepare examples that show how you have successfully balanced competing priorities without losing quality or dropping commitments.

- **Communication skills:** At its core, DevRel is about communication. A good advocate can make complex ideas clear without making the audience feel talked down to. Interviews will test this, often by asking you to explain a technical concept to a non-technical audience. Employers want to see that you can listen as well as explain, and that you adapt your message to the person in front of you. Think of examples from your own experience—whether it was writing documentation, teaching a coworker, or presenting at a meetup—that demonstrate your ability to communicate with clarity and empathy.

- **Technical credibility:** Finally, credibility matters. You do not need to be the most senior engineer in the room, but you need to be able to reason about APIs, SDKs, authentication flows, and trade-offs, and to talk through them with confidence. Many interviews will include coding questions or scenario-based exercises, such as explaining a concept like OAuth to an executive or writing a short piece of sample documentation. Employers are looking for evidence that you can both build with the tools and explain them to others, bridging the gap between product and developer. In preparation, it's worth brushing up on language skills. It's impossible to be 100% prepared for every possible technical question regarding any software language. To help focus your preparation, start off by looking up the "best" interview questions for the specific languages the role requires. This will help cover the basics. Afterward, take a deep dive into the company's products, SDKs, and APIs and re-familiarize yourself with any structures, algorithms, and third-party packages that would be needed to successfully deploy those products.

8.4.3 Prepare for the DevRel Interview Loop

Unlike traditional engineering interviews, DevRel interviews are highly varied. They test your technical skills, communication ability, and advocacy mindset all at once. To piece together what candidates can expect, I've drawn from three places: the personal accounts of advocates who have shared their experiences, published hiring processes from companies like PostHog, Warp, and Retool, and my own experience interviewing and hiring for these roles.

While every company does things differently, a typical loop might include:

Culture or Screening Interview

These early calls are usually with HR or a hiring manager. Companies use this to check alignment on mission, communication style, and growth mindset. They focus on whether you understand the role, the company, and why you want to move into DevRel. You might be asked about your background, your motivations, or what excites you about the product. It helps to show that you've researched the company and its community, and that you have thought about how you can contribute.

Be ready to explain why DevRel appeals to you and why this company in particular stands out. This is also the time to ask your own questions, such as "Who owns the vision for developer relations here?" or "How do you see this role evolving over the next year?"

Technical Interview

Unlike an engineering interview, you are not usually asked to implement an algorithm on a whiteboard. Instead, you might

- Solve a coding challenge that demonstrates problem-solving and clarity, not just correctness

- Write or review a sample of documentation

- Explain a technical concept to a specific audience (e.g., "Explain REST APIs to a room of designers" or "Explain containers to the CEO of a small consultancy"). You'd be expected to tailor your answer to the specific audience by clarifying what that audience already knows and then framing your answer to their level.

This stage tests both your technical credibility and your ability to adapt to different audiences, which is a core part of advocacy. Google, for example, is known to keep a high bar for coding ability in DevRel engineering roles, but they weigh clarity of thought and communication just as heavily as correctness.

Content or Communication Task

Nearly every DevRel loop includes a content task. You may be asked to draft a tutorial for a fictional API, record a short video demo, outline a blog post, or deliver a presentation. The goal is to see how you teach, structure information, and empathize with developers who are learning.

A common variation is being asked to present the same concept to two different audiences, such as junior developers and executives. Strong candidates anticipate where someone might get stuck and frame their content to help them succeed. Reviewers want to see that you can break down problems in ways that are accessible, accurate, and engaging.

Take-Home Assignment

Some companies, like Warp and Retool, use a take-home to simulate the actual work. This might involve designing a content plan, writing a tutorial, or sketching a strategy for growing a community. PostHog even runs a paid "SuperDay" where candidates spend a full day working with the team on a real-world task.

The key here is not polish but thought process. They want to see how you approach problems, how you prioritize, and how you communicate decisions. It'd help to remember to keep scope manageable and make your reasoning explicit. Make it clear why you chose a topic, why you used a particular format, what trade-offs you considered.

Go the extra mile, especially if it's your first DevRel role. You could create a video to accompany your submission. A certain manager mentioned how candidates who sent along videos to explain their answers were always at the top of his list. These videos don't have to be professionally done either, just your voice over a screen recording as you walk through your project.

Not only do these videos provide insights into your thought process and existing skillsets, they showcase how you'll come across when doing this for the company. Presenting at conferences, webinars, and workshops are all common asks for an experienced advocate. If you don't have recent recordings of doing this, then I highly recommend creating these videos.

Final Round/Team Fit

This stage is usually cross-functional. You might speak with engineers, product managers, marketing, or executives. They are evaluating how you will work across the company and represent it externally. Expect questions like

- "Tell us about a time you gave feedback to a product team. What happened?"

- "How would you handle a developer publicly criticizing our product on Twitter?"

- "What excites you about our roadmap, and what concerns you?"

Think through stories from your past experience that show collaboration, empathy, and problem-solving.

Prepare thoughtful questions for each group (e.g., to engineering: "How does DevRel currently contribute to improving DX?" to leadership: "What's the biggest opportunity for DevRel to impact the business?"). And, be honest about what you enjoy and what you don't. A good fit is mutual.

Other Common Questions to Expect

- **"How would you handle a developer publicly criticizing our product on Twitter?"**

   Here, the interviewer is looking for empathy and professionalism. A strong answer begins with acknowledging the frustration, rather than dismissing it. You can then suggest moving the conversation to a constructive channel, like a forum or DM, to gather facts and work toward resolution. Once the issue is fixed, it's important to close the loop publicly so others see the company takes feedback seriously.

- **"What makes great docs or APIs?"**

  This tests your technical credibility and your understanding of developer experience. Focus on concrete qualities: clear structure, runnable quickstarts, meaningful error messages, good versioning, and well-maintained changelogs. Strengthen your answer by pointing to one example you admire and explaining why it stands out, whether it's Stripe's documentation for its copy-and-paste code snippets or Twilio's sample apps that reduce setup time.

- **"How do you decide what content to produce?"**

  Interviewers want to know that your choices are guided by developer need, not personal preference. Good answers show that you draw input from community sources like GitHub issues, Stack Overflow questions, roadmap priorities, or search trends. Then tie your content decisions back to outcomes: Does it reduce time to first success? Does it unblock common pain points?

- **"How do you measure success in DevRel?"**

  This question probes whether you can link your work to impact. A thoughtful answer connects your work to the four pillars of DevRel: awareness (reach and impressions), education (time to first success, course completions), community (answered questions, sentiment), and feedback (product changes shipped as a result). Always frame metrics in terms of developer outcomes rather than vanity numbers.

- **"Walk me through a project end to end."**

  The interviewer is testing both execution and reflection. Structure your story around the problem, the audience, your plan, execution, results, and lessons learned. Include at least one number and one piece of feedback to anchor your answer. For example: "I built a tutorial series that reached 5,000 developers and received feedback from three who said it helped them finish onboarding in half the time."

- **"What do you hope to learn by joining our team?"**

  This isn't really about five-year plans. It's about curiosity and alignment. Employers want to see that you're eager to grow in areas relevant to their work, whether that's deepening skills with APIs, learning about community programs, or expanding into new technical domains. Keep your answer grounded in the team's context rather than abstract career aspirations.

- **"How do you stay up-to-date with tech?"**

  This reveals whether you balance curiosity with discernment. A good response mentions specific sources you follow, such as newsletters, open-source communities, or side projects, but also how you filter out noise. For instance, you might say you track trends in AI or developer tooling but only dive deep when you see consistent adoption patterns.

- **"Who do you think will be our next competitor?"**

  Here they're checking if you've studied the ecosystem. Strong candidates mention both the obvious competitors and smaller emerging players, then explain why those matter. Your reasoning is more important than naming the "right" company.

- **"What are the next big technology trends?"**

  This is about your ability to think long term. Instead of pointing to the latest JavaScript framework, frame your answer in broader categories like AI, edge computing, or real-time collaboration. Add one or two specific trends you personally follow and explain why they're significant.

- **"How would you evaluate whether to sponsor an event?"**

  This question tests whether you understand trade-offs in community programs. Good answers cover attendee demographics, sponsorship cost versus reach, whether the event skews commercial or community-driven, and what outcomes the company expects, whether that's leads, brand visibility, or stronger community ties.

- **"How do you measure the success of a conference talk or booth?"**

  They want to see if you can think beyond headcount. Mention metrics like attendance, questions asked, and social shares, but also point to qualitative wins, such as developer quotes or follow-up conversations that led to adoption.

`Startup.jobs` has a resource with more developer advocacy interview questions you can practice with, here: `https://startup.jobs/interview-questions/developer-advocate966`

8.4.4 Prepare Your Own Questions for the Team

Interviews are a two-way street. Having no questions of your own can come across as disinterest and may be a red flag for employers.

The company is assessing whether you can represent their product and community, but you should also be assessing whether this role will set you up for success. Good questions help you uncover what the job is really like day to day, how the team operates, and whether the organization values developer relations beyond the buzzwords. Tailor your list depending on who you are speaking to, whether that's your potential manager, teammates, or executives. Prepare a short list for each person in your loop. Open-ended questions reveal culture and expectations.

Here are sample questions you could ask:

HR or Talent

- How do you level advocates here and what does growth look like over 12 to 24 months?

- How much vacation do people actually take and how is time off encouraged?

Hiring manager

- How do you measure DevRel success for this role and how often do you review it?

- Where does DevRel sit in the org and how do you collaborate with Product and Engineering?

- What is the biggest community or DX problem you want this hire to tackle first?

Future Teammates

- What does a typical week look like across content, community, feedback, and travel?

- Which parts of the program are working well and which need rethinking?

- How often do you ship together across time zones and how do you handle on-call for the community?

Product or Engineering

- Can you share an example of developer feedback that changed the roadmap?

- How do you prefer to receive and prioritize community feedback?

Leadership

- What is the clearest path for DevRel to move business metrics this year?

- What will convince you that DevRel should grow headcount next year?

Community-Specific Probes

- Who is the vision keeper for the community program?

- Describe your community as a product. Where does it live, what are the core features, and what does it cost to run?

- What is the Venn diagram between community, audience, and customer here?

8.4.5 Watch Out for Red Flags

Not every DevRel opportunity is healthy. The role is constantly evolving, and some companies do not fully understand or support advocacy. Joining one of these teams can leave you frustrated, overworked, or burnt out. Because DevRel is highly visible and autonomous, it is easy for companies to misuse it, expecting one person to do everything. Be alert for warning signs in the interview process. A healthy DevRel job should stretch you without draining you. If a company expects you to sacrifice rest, boundaries, or your personal life, that's a sign to step away. Some common red flags include

- **Vague success metrics:** If a company cannot clearly explain how they measure DevRel success, expect confusion and misalignment once you join

- **Leadership without DevRel experience:** When senior leaders oversimplify the work or treat it as "just tweeting and speaking," they are unlikely to give you the support you need. If they cannot articulate what day-to-day value you are expected to deliver, they probably don't understand the function. Also, if they indicate no plans of growing or investing in the team if you're joining as a first hire, that's problematic.

- **Unrealistic scope:** Be cautious if one role combines content creation, community management, events, support, and product feedback without any prioritization. That usually signals a lack of focus and risk of burnout.

- **Toxic work culture:** Expect trouble if you hear about 24/7 availability, pressure to work through weekends or nights across time zones, or managers punishing you for taking recovery time after travel. Or expecting you to work straight through multi-day trips without compensatory time off.

Of course, occasional crunch moments are part of the job. Launches and conferences will stretch you. But it shouldn't be a pattern.

- **Lack of growth trajectory:** A healthy DevRel role should have clear milestones for career progression: what success looks like, when your performance will be reviewed, and how promotions, title changes, and pay increases are handled. If a company cannot describe what advancement looks like, or if they wave away the question by saying "we'll figure it out later," that usually means there is no plan. Without a roadmap for your growth, you risk staying stuck at the same level while carrying more and more responsibility.

To spot these issues early, ask targeted questions in the interview:

- How much vacation does the average employee take? Do you enforce a minimum number of days off per year? (Secret: a lot of "unlimited vacation day" policies actually lead to employees taking less time off because they feel guilty.)

- How often do team members work beyond expected hours?

- What are the expectations for asynchronous communication? Do you expect me to respond immediately to Slack messages from coworkers? Am I expected to be available 24/7? (Spoilers: that should be no!)

- How does the team treat travel days? Are they considered work or extra? Traveling is stressful and should be considered work.

- How do promotions and pay raises work on this team? Is there a timeline or framework you follow?

- What does career progression look like for this role over the next two to three years?

- Can you share an example of someone on the DevRel team who has grown into a more senior role? What steps did they take and how was their growth supported?

No matter how badly you want a job, if you get a bad feeling about any of this, swipe left and move along. Find a job at a company that values you!

Summary

Getting into DevRel is less about credentials and more about proof. A portfolio that demonstrates how you can analyze developer needs, design a strategy, create content, and measure results is more convincing than any title. When you pair this with a resume tailored to highlight your communication, teaching, and community experience, you give hiring managers a clear story of how you already practice the work.

That story also needs to be visible in the right places. Opportunities in DevRel often surface through networks, communities, and advocates sharing leads rather than through traditional job boards. By showing your work publicly and engaging with peers, you not only build credibility but also increase your chances of hearing about roles before they're formally announced.

When those opportunities lead to interviews, you'll face conversations designed to test the dual nature of advocacy: technical credibility and the ability to teach, empathize, and adapt on the fly. The best preparation is practice—writing, speaking, and engaging in communities—so you can draw on concrete stories that reveal how you think and how you connect with developers.

Even with preparation, not every role is worth accepting. Vague expectations, lack of growth paths, or cultures that glorify overwork are warning signs that the environment may not sustain you. The best DevRel roles give you clarity, balance, and room to grow.

In the next chapter, we'll turn to what comes after the offer: how to navigate your first 90 days and lay the foundation for long-term success as a developer advocate.

CHAPTER 9

Your First 90 Days As a Developer Advocate

Up until this point, we've gone through everything you need to know to land a developer advocacy role, and now you've actually landed one.

Congratulations. Really, take a moment to celebrate that. But as exciting as this milestone is, the truth is the real work starts here.

The first 90 days are critical. They shape how you're perceived, whether you make it past probation, and how well you set yourself up for long-term success. Done right, they create momentum that carries you forward, open doors to strong relationships across the company, and set the tone for the rest of your time there. Done poorly, they can leave you struggling to prove your value.

This chapter is about getting those first 90 days right. We'll talk about how to build momentum early, how to form the relationships that will support your work, and how to leave people saying, "We're so glad we hired you." Think of it as a playbook for turning your first three months into the foundation for everything that follows.

To bring in a fresh, practical perspective, I reached out to my friend Edidiong Asikpo, who at the time of writing had just wrapped up her probation as a Developer Advocate at MongoDB. Beyond her professional

269
L. Ikechukwu, *A Friendly Guide to Developer Advocacy*, Friendly Guides to Technology,
https://doi.org/10.1007/979-8-8688-2462-3_9

role, Edidiong is also a core team member of Open Source Community Africa, the organizers of one of the largest annual gatherings of open source professionals and enthusiasts on the continent. Her insights are especially valuable because they come straight from the experience of having just gone through her own first 90 days.

By the end of 90 days, you want to be able to say: here's what I've learned about our developers, here's what I've shipped, here's the feedback I've collected, and here's where I think we should go next.

9.1 Week 1: Learn and Build Camaraderie

When you step into a new DevRel role, it is important to remember that while the overarching goals are usually the same—driving awareness and adoption—what that actually looks like is always different from company to company. What worked at one company may not work at another, because every organization has its own expectations, culture, and way of defining success. Do not assume that your role or DevRel as a whole will function the same way as it did in your previous job.

The first thing you should do in your first week is to understand exactly what you are expected to accomplish. Some of this may have been discussed during your interview, but this is the time to dive deeper into alignment and secure concrete buy-in and agreement.

Everything discussed in Chapter 4 comes in handy here. You want to understand the company, the product, who the product is for, and the team you will be working with. To begin, read public company documents such as guides, guidelines, and help docs. Study product material, especially benchmarking reports, to understand the market and competitors. Learn about the tools your team and company use. Get access to them and become familiar. Beyond written materials, the best way to gain insight is from the people already working there.

Ask your manager to introduce you to key leaders, teammates, and anyone whose work intersects with yours. These are the people who will shape your success: engineering, product, marketing, sales, customer support, and the DevRel team, if one exists. Because your job will touch many teams, it is crucial to build cross-functional relationships early.

For each of these meetings, which should last no more than an hour, keep the following talking points in mind:

> **Learn about the individual:** Ask about their background, strengths, personality, and preferred communication style. Learn their goals, what they are currently working on, and how they see the role of developer advocacy in the company.

> **Let them learn about you:** Use these conversations to build credibility and respect. Explain your background, what you have been hired to do, and how your work might support theirs. Not everyone will understand what an advocate does, so this is your chance to position your role clearly.

> **Look for opportunities for early wins:** Ask where they think your strengths would be best applied, or what they believe could count as a quick win for you, or one thing you can do based on your role that would immediately make their work easier. Many may not have an answer, but some will. Use their feedback to identify potential areas where you can ship something tangible in your first month.

Some companies may tell you to take your time, but do not. Hit the ground running. Your first month shapes how people see you, and those early impressions are valuable. You want colleagues to notice your contributions quickly and begin rooting for you. A visible early win boosts your confidence, signals that you can execute, and creates goodwill that compounds over time.

Helpful questions to ask include

- "What's one thing you wish had been in place when you first joined?"

- "Where do you think developer experience could be better today?"

- "What do you love most about the company?"

- "What areas do you feel need improvement?"

- What are the top 3 recurring gotchas, confusing steps, or error patterns you see?

Beyond the general questions you'll ask everyone, certain teams are knowledge holders for specific information that will help you understand the product, the company, the community, and the market. If you want your strategy to be grounded, you need to know who to ask for what.

9.1.1 Marketing

Marketing usually holds the clearest picture of how the company positions itself in the market. If you're joining an established company, they'll likely have already defined the ideal customer profile (ICP), segments, and positioning. If you're joining a younger company without a formal marketing team, those answers might live with the founders or early product leaders—and sometimes you'll need to figure them out yourself.

Questions to ask marketing:

- How do we define our ideal customer profile? Who is our best-fit developer and company, and who are we not trying to serve?

- Which developer segments or personas are the highest priority right now?

- What external market drivers matter most for us—new regulations, AI trends, platform shifts?

- What story do we tell to developers that differentiates us from alternatives?

- Which SEO keywords, campaigns, or narratives are the highest priority this quarter?

- What proof assets are missing that DevRel could help create (integration guides, case studies, quickstarts, comparison content)?

9.1.2 Sales

Sales is where you'll learn how customers actually evaluate your product against competitors. They see what closes deals, what stalls them, and what technical objections come up again and again.

Questions to ask sales:

- In won deals, who tends to be the initiator, implementer, influencer, and approver?

- What objections or blockers do you hear most often from each of those roles?

- Who do we most often lose to, and why? What do prospects say those competitors do better?

- Which proof points or technical content help close deals? Which ones are missing?

- What competitive comparisons or migration guides would be most useful in the field?

- For the top two reasons teams switch to us, what artifacts are missing (migration guides, side-by-side code snippets, "before/after" blog)?

9.1.3 Product

Product management holds the vision for what the company is building and why. They know the product category, where it sits in the stack, and what's coming next.

Questions to ask product:

- What product category are we in (API, SDK, service, platform), and what baseline developer experience expectations come with that category?

- Which segments and use cases are we prioritizing this quarter?

- What assumptions are we making about the typical user's environment, language, or skill level?

- What kinds of companies or teams is the product designed for—and where does it not fit?

- What are the top friction points surfaced by telemetry, beta feedback, or support tickets?

- How should DevRel feed developer insights back into the roadmap?

9.1.4 Engineering

Engineering is where you'll uncover how the product actually feels to use. They'll know the quirks, technical debt, and places where developers get stuck.

Questions to ask engineering:

- What is the fastest path from "hello world" to a meaningful outcome with our product? How long does it typically take?

- What parts of the developer experience cause the most confusion (SDKs, error messages, docs)?

- Which integrations, frameworks, or platforms matter most right now?

- Where do breaking changes hit users hardest, and how do we help developers migrate?

- What internal benchmarks or performance data can we safely share with the outside world?

You can even ask an engineer to help demo and explain how the product works to you.

9.1.5 Customer Success/Support

Customer success is often closest to real users. They know where people drop off in onboarding, what frustrates them, and what keeps them happy.

Questions to ask customer success:

- What are the most frequent tickets or questions you see from developers?

- Where do trials stall (permissions, networking, quotas, SDK confusion)? What quickstart or checklist would reduce time-to-value?

- What features are hardest for users to adopt or understand?

- What behaviors predict renewal/expansion? What education correlates with those behaviors?

- What content or walkthroughs would make your work easier and prevent common tickets?

9.1.6 Other DevRel Team Members

If you're joining an established DevRel team, your peers are your best shortcut into what's already working. You want to find out from them what areas they feel are lacking and need improvement. Where do they think they were already doing well before you joined? What are their immediate expectations of you?

Questions to ask your DevRel colleagues:

- Which content formats or channels have proven most impactful here? Which ones don't move the needle?

- Which developer cohorts respond best to our work? Which ones are low-yield?

- What metrics leadership pays most attention to when evaluating DevRel?

- What projects would you double down on if you had more bandwidth?

It might also be important to try and schedule meetings with all relevant leaders to ask about their team's goals, then ask what their vision of the Developer Advocate role is in the organization, and align expectations.

Don't forget to document everything you learn from these meetings. Didi keeps a file called devrelat[company].doc where she notes every personal information, expectation, request, and insight from each person. This document would be divided into sections with headers of individual names of the people she spoke with. This prevents misalignment, gives you something to revisit when you feel lost, and makes it easier to check progress later with your manager.

9.2 Week 2: Draft Your Plan

By your second week, you've had a round of introductory conversations, asked questions, and uncovered pain points, opportunities, and gaps. Now it's time to make sense of what you've learned and begin turning it into a plan.

Start by creating a document where you list all the insights you've gathered: the pain points surfaced in your conversations, opportunities for improvement, gaps in the developer experience, and suggestions people shared with you. This becomes your working inventory of possible projects.

There will still be a lot to learn—about the product, the tools, the processes, and the community —to catch up. The temptation is to stay in learning mode until you feel "ready." That is the fastest way to trap yourself in what developers call tutorial hell.

Instead, structure your learning around execution or *just-in-time learning*, first popularized in software engineering and education, and inspired by lean manufacturing's idea of "just-in-time production."

Research in educational psychology has shown that learning tied to immediate, meaningful application sticks better than information absorbed in the abstract. You learn faster, you retain more, and you avoid cognitive overload.

For every deliverable, there will be knowledge gaps you must close to complete it. Focus on those. If you are working on documentation, you'd need to learn how the docs system is structured while fixing a real issue. If you are preparing a demo, you need to learn the product's integration points by actually building with them. Each task becomes both an output and a learning opportunity, and over time, these incremental steps compound into true proficiency without overwhelming you with information overload.

Your company might give you an onboarding plan, or it might not. And when an onboarding plan is provided, it usually focuses on setup and integration: getting your laptop configured, installing the necessary apps, learning the org chart, and meeting the team. What it often does not include are outcome-driven deliverables tied directly to your role. If that's the case, you need to work with your manager to shape and agree on what your deliverables should be for your first 90 days.

Bring your collection of pain points and opportunities to the conversation and ask:

- Which company KPIs should my work ladder to?

- What is the north-star reason I was hired?

- If I can only accomplish three things in my first 90 days, whether from this list or not, what are they, and what should I explicitly not do?

- What evidence will we use to call my work successful?

From that conversation, agree on and define three categories of focus or deliverables for your first 90 days:

Quick Win (end of Month 1): A quick win is a small but visible deliverable you can ship by the end of your first month. It should be valuable to the company, achievable within a few weeks, and noticeable enough that others see the impact. Quick wins build momentum, shape how people perceive you, and give you an early boost of confidence.

However, you don't have to wait until the end of Month 1 to put out something. While your first quick win is the formal deliverable you agree on, by the end of week 2, you can make smaller early contributions, such as posting on social channels about what you're learning, sharing surprising insights about the tool or ecosystem, or drafting a short article documenting your experiences while beginning to build with the product. These mini wins help you get started, gain visibility, and lay the foundation for your larger quick win.

When you join, people may tell you to take your time. Don't. Hit the ground running. Early wins set the tone for your entire probation period. They demonstrate that you can make decisions, deliver results, and create value quickly. They get people excited about your joining and establish goodwill that compounds over time. A visible win in your first month not only signals capability but also encourages colleagues to root for your success.

This first quick win also does not need to be a major project. It could be as simple as fixing a documentation issue, running an SEO keyword analysis, or setting up a system for prioritizing topics. The important thing is to ship something by the end of your first month.

For example, Edidiong was hired to move developer conversations from MongoDB-owned private forums to third-party spaces like Stack Overflow and Reddit. Her early win could be identifying five active communities where MongoDB-related topics were already being discussed, seeding ten conversations, and involving engineers in answering questions.

2 Primary Outcomes for Months 2 and 3 (PKR1 and PKR2): These are directly tied to the reason you were hired. They should be meaningful, achievable within two months, and aligned with your core responsibilities or the north star goal for hiring you. For example, if you were hired to improve onboarding, a primary deliverable might be reducing the number of support tickets tied to setup issues.

Secondary outcome or key result (SKR): These are about building relationships and showing you are a team player. They may not sit at the heart of your role, but they make you visible across the company. For instance, helping marketing adapt a blog post into a developer-friendly Twitter thread, or supporting customer success with a technical FAQ. Look for ways to lighten other people's load; even small contributions like drafting a post or reviewing content. These gestures build goodwill and ensure that when you need support, colleagues will show up for you.

To ground this in an example: imagine you join a developer tools startup.

- From engineering, you hear that developers struggle with the setup script.

- From sales, you learn that a competitor is winning deals on ease of use.

From support, you see repeated tickets about deployment errors.

- From customer success, you learn that developers frequently complain about a confusing onboarding step.

- The marketing team is trying to grow the company's presence on Twitter but lacks developer-focused content and the audience, but you have a healthy developer following on twitter and LinkedIn.

Now you know that for your company, DevRel's objective or north-star mission is to offer the best onboarding experience in your market segment in order to improve acquisition and retention. This is where the work you did in Chapter 5 on defining OKRs comes in handy.

You want to make sure that your deliverables and key results tie back to the company's or overall DevRel objective. That way you're not just working in isolation, but directly contributing to the strategy.

Based on the opportunities identified above, these may be your selections:

- **Quick win (Month 1):** Publish a new quickstart guide that smooths out setup.

- **Primary outcome 1 (Month 2):** Document the top five deployment errors and fixes.

- **Primary outcome 2 (Month 3):** Create a sales enablement post showcasing ease of use over a competitor.

- **Secondary outcome:** Repurpose your onboarding work into developer-focused Twitter threads for marketing on Fridays.

Once you've defined your quick win, primary and secondary deliverables, the next step is to work backward to break each one down into smaller tasks that cascade into the final output, so that you can estimate a timeline for delivery and also keep yourself accountable and engaged and also offers a way to track your progress. Breaking down outcomes into tasks not only makes them less overwhelming but also gives you checkpoints to share with your manager.

Start from the deliverable you want to ship and ask: what needs to be true for me to complete this? Then ask the same question for each sub-task until you reach the smallest actionable pieces.

Let's take one example deliverable: **Publish a new quickstart guide that smooths out setup by the end of Month 1.**

Walking backward might look like this:

1. **Deliverable:** Publish a quickstart guide.

   - For this to happen, you need the final content reviewed and approved.

2. **Step back:** Content ready for review.

   - Tasks: Write the first draft. Share with engineering for technical accuracy. Share with the design or docs team for formatting.

3. **Step back:** Draft written.

   - Tasks: Outline the quickstart flow. Decide what language or framework you'll use. Gather code snippets. Test the flow end-to-end.

4. **Step back:** Outline created.

   - Tasks: Audit existing onboarding docs. Identify common friction points from conversations with customer success and support. Decide which part of the setup experience the guide will address.

5. **Step back:** Friction points identified.

   - Tasks: Review support tickets. Revisit notes from Week 1 interviews. Test the setup script yourself in a clean environment. Note where things break or cause confusion.

See how every step feeds the next? By breaking it down this way, you now have a sequence of learning-and-doing tasks that get you to the deliverable, from which you can now estimate your timeline for delivery. So you might have something like

- Review tickets and interview notes (1 day)

- Test setup on a clean environment (1 day)

- Outline quickstart and get buy-in (2 days)

- Write draft with code snippets (3 days)

- Peer review and revisions (2–3 days)

- Final formatting and publishing (1 day)

Edidiong emphasized the importance of building in buffers into your timeline estimates. Right now, the task above is estimated to take about 10 days. You should add a buffer of 2 to 5 days, that way you've built in margin for unexpected delays, and if you deliver in 10, you've exceeded expectations. It's always better to under-promise and over-deliver than the reverse, which gradually erodes trust in your capacity. And if for any reason, something happens to delay your delivery, you want to practice proactive communication.

Now you want to take all of this and set up a work plan or diary that will guide you. This could be as simple as a google doc or a notion page. List tasks for each day according to your timeline and be sure to leave spaces for notes on each day to document what you learned or stuff. Keeping track of your tasks this way can even go a long way to being something you reference when performance review comes around and also for when you need to look back on your work achievements.

Something like Figure 9-1 below:

Work Diary 2025

▼ SEPTEMBER: **Publish a New Quickstart Guide**

Monday, Sept 15

☐ Review onboarding feedback from support tickets.

☐ Revisit notes from Week 1 conversations.

☐ Decide on the specific flow that the QuickStart will fix.

Notes:

Tuesday, Sept 16

☐ Test setup in a clean environment.

☐ Identify top friction points in setup

Notes:

Wednesday, Sept 17

☐ Audit existing documentation for overlaps or gaps.

☐ Draft initial QuickStart outline.

Notes:

Thursday, Sept 18

☐ Share outline with manager and engineers for input.

☐ Revise outline based on feedback.

☐ Test setup in a clean environment.

Notes:

Friday, Sept 19

☐ Collect sample code snippets to include in the guide.

☐ Test snippets to confirm they work end-to-end.

Notes:

Figure 9-1. *Sample work plan diary*

9.3 Weeks 3 and 4: Ship and Share Your First Win

By your third week, the focus shifts from planning to execution. You have already gathered insights, aligned with your manager, and selected your deliverables. Now it is time to secure your first quick win and make it visible.

When you ship your first win—whether it is a quickstart guide, a set of seeded community conversations, or a fix to a recurring documentation issue—share it directly with your manager. Frame it as: here is what I delivered, here is why it matters, and here is what I am tracking to measure its effect. From there, broaden the visibility. Post an update in the relevant team channel, whether that is DevRel, marketing, product, or even company-wide, if appropriate. Your update does not need to be long.

A short message works: *This month I worked on X, here is what shipped, and next month I plan to focus on Y. If this overlaps with your work or if you would like to be kept in the loop, let me know.* Be sure to tag colleagues who supported you, as it not only gives credit but also shows that you collaborate across functions, and promotes your visibility to the broader team.

Promoting your visibility is important for your growth and recognition, because while your manager may know what you are doing, the rest of the company often does not. Visibility creates perception. You want people outside your immediate team to see the value you are adding. The alternative is being busy but invisible.

In my first year at Smallstep, for instance, I spent months writing documentation and creating sales enablement material, but outside the marketing team, nobody knew. At a retreat, an engineer asked me, "So what do you do for the company?" That moment underscored the importance of being vocal about my work. Do not repeat my mistake. Make visibility a habit from the start.

Week 4 is also your chance to introduce your first monthly review with your manager. Think of this as a structured checkpoint beyond your weekly one-on-ones. In this session, look back on what you accomplished in your first month, how it connects to the company's priorities, and whether it delivered the impact you intended. Then look forward: confirm with your manager what your focus should be for the next month, and check that it still aligns with the company's evolving needs.

Ask simple, open questions such as "How do you think I'm doing?" or "What would you like me to adjust?" These reviews will prevent surprises at the end of your probation and give you clarity and confidence about your direction.

9.4 Months 2 and 3: Execute and Expand

With your quick win behind you, the next phase is about sustained execution. These two months are when you demonstrate not just that you can deliver but that you can deliver consistently. Return to the two primary outcomes you agreed on with your manager.

As you work, keep a running log of friction points and opportunities you uncover. One of the advantages you have as a newcomer is a fresh perspective. You will notice inefficiencies and gaps that others may overlook because they have grown used to them. Document these insights. Some may turn into future projects beyond your first 90 days. Others may simply give you useful talking points with your manager or your peers. Either way, they reinforce your value as someone who sees clearly and speaks up.

Execution is not only about doing the work but also about sustaining the habits of communication you established in Month 1. Keep your manager and collaborators looped in. Share status updates. When you reach milestones—publishing a doc, launching a tutorial, running a workshop—communicate them the same way you did with your quick win: here is what shipped, and here is how it connects to the company's goals.

By the end of each month, hold another review session with your manager. These reviews are more than status updates. They are structured checkpoints where you

- **Look back**: What did you ship? What was the impact? Did it meet the definition of success you agreed on?

- **Look ahead**: What will you focus on next month? Does it still align with the company's evolving needs?

- **Invite feedback**: Ask directly, "How do you think I'm doing?" or "Is there anything you'd like me to adjust?"

These conversations build trust and reduce uncertainty. They also give you a clear sense of whether you are on track to pass probation.

By the end of Month 3, you should have two substantial deliverables shipped, a track record of visible contributions, and a reputation as someone who not only executes but also collaborates. These months are where you shift from "the new hire finding their footing" to "a valuable teammate who is clearly moving the company forward."

9.5 Week 12: Reflect, Report, and Reset

You should aim to ship your last planned deliverable no later than Week 11, so that by Week 12 you have the space to reflect and create a report that ties everything together.

Start by reviewing the outcomes you committed to in your first 90 days. What did you ship? How did it perform? Did it meet the success criteria you and your manager agreed on? Frame your report around how your actions contributed to KPIs that connect back to the north-star reason for your role. Everything you learned in Chapter 7 about measuring impact and metrics will be useful here.

If you were hired to improve onboarding, show how your work reduced friction, led to fewer complaints, or made the product easier to adopt. If your mandate was visibility, show how your contributions expanded awareness or drove more external engagement. The key is to connect the dots between your activities and the company's priorities. Alignment and impact are what leaders look for.

Depending on your activities, here are some relevant KPIs you may want to highlight:

- **Support Efficiency**: Did repeated questions in support decrease after new documentation or tutorials went live?

- **Content Reach and Engagement**: Did your blog post or guide generate traffic, spark social media responses, or get referenced in other blog posts, newsletters, or podcasts?

- **Community Impact**: Did your seeded conversations lead to ongoing threads, community-generated answers, or adoption in forums like Stack Overflow or Reddit?

- **Product Influence**: How many issues, feature requests, or roadmap decisions were shaped by developer feedback you collected and shared?

- **Developer Adoption**: Did published content, tutorials, or workshops lead to sign-ups, activations, or measurable usage?

- **Sales Enablement**: Did sales teams use your blog post, demo, or FAQ in conversations with customers? How many deals did it support or unblock?

- **Event or Awareness Outcomes**: Did your content or community work lead to invitations for webinars, sponsorships, or external collaborations?

After sharing this report with your manager, post a concise version in your team's public channels. Visibility is not self-promotion—it is a way of reinforcing impact across the company. A short message like "In my first 90 days I shipped X and Y, which led to Z outcomes, and next I'll be focusing on..." keeps colleagues in the loop and strengthens your reputation as someone who delivers.

End the review by using these insights to reset your direction. Bring your notes on gaps and opportunities you noticed, and work with your manager to shape your next 90-day outcomes. The cycle then begins again: define deliverables, walk them backward, and execute with learning built into the process

This cycle of visibility and reporting serves another purpose in equipping your manager with evidence when the time comes to argue for your probation pass, or later for a promotion. They won't need to scramble for proof of your impact. Your track record will already be documented and visible, supported by metrics that tie directly to business value.

Summary

The first 90 days in developer advocacy set the foundation for your long-term success. In this chapter, we explored how to listen deeply, align with your manager, define meaningful deliverables, and ship visible outcomes that build trust.

You learned how to balance execution with learning, how to avoid getting trapped in endless preparation, and how to create momentum through early wins. We also covered the habits of visibility, feedback, and reflection that will carry you far beyond your probation period.

Unfortunately, this chapter also marks the close of the book. Across these nine chapters, we've walked through the full arc of developer advocacy: what it is, why it matters, how to design impactful programs, the formats that bring it to life, and the metrics that prove its value. We've looked at strategy, execution, community, content, code, and the personal skills needed to thrive in a role that sits at the intersection of product, engineering, marketing, and people. We looked at how to enter the field, how to land a role, and how to thrive once you are in.

As you step into—or continue—the journey of advocacy, remember that growth comes from doing. Learn by building, experiment openly, and treat each cycle of execution and reflection as a chance to get sharper. Stay visible. Keep listening. Measure what matters. And above all, hold on to the curiosity and empathy that drew you here in the first place.

I end the book here, but this is just the beginning. You now have the tools, frameworks, and examples to navigate your journey with confidence. The next chapters are yours to write. Write them well.

Appendix

Success Metrics Definitions

- **Call-to-Action (CTA) Conversion Rate (Blogs):**
  Measures the percentage of blog visitors who click
  a contextual CTA within the post (e.g., "Download
  the SDK", "Subscribe to our newsletter", or "Join our
  community"). This matters because it proves the blog
  post is effective in driving a high-value next step toward
  adoption or community membership.

- **Pages Per Session (Blogs):** Measures the average
  number of pages a reader visits on your site after
  reading the blog post. This matters because it
  indicates high interest and successful internal linking,
  showing the blog post is an effective entry point to
  documentation or other content.

- **Inbound Links/Backlinks (Blogs):** Measures the
  number of other reputable, third-party sites (especially
  other developers or tech blogs) that link to your post.
  This matters because it's a strong proxy for authority
  and thought leadership, showing that other experts
  vouch for your content's technical credibility.

L. Ikechukwu, *A Friendly Guide to Developer Advocacy*, Friendly Guides to Technology,
https://doi.org/10.1007/979-8-8688-2462-3

- **Scroll Depth (Blogs):** Measures how far down the page users scroll (e.g., 75% or 90% completion). This matters because it tells you if developers are actually consuming the full technical depth of the content, which is more insightful than simple page views.

- **Social Shares and Engagement (Blogs):** Measures the volume of likes, comments, and shares on social media posts that link to the blog. This matters because it measures the content's inherent value and virality, proving it is useful enough for developers to endorse and share with their networks.

- **No. of Registrations (Webinars/Hackathons):** Measures the total number of people who signed up for the event. This matters because it measures top-of-funnel awareness and marketing reach and is used for predicting attendance and planning.

- **No. of Attendees (Webinars/Hackathons):** Measures the total number of people who actually showed up for and consumed the content. This matters because it measures the quality of the lead generation and the perceived value of the content promised in the promotion.

- **Repo Forks/Code Usage (Webinars/Hackathons):** Measures the number of attendees who fork a provided code repository or successfully complete a guided code-along/challenge. This matters because it tracks the transition from learning to active building, proving the event accelerated **Time to Value (TTV).**

- **Question-to-Attendee Ratio (Webinars/Hackathons):**
  Measures the total number of unique questions asked
  in Q&A divided by the number of attendees. This
  matters because it indicates active participation and
  high engagement, and is a useful way to quickly identify
  product friction points or content gaps.

- **Time to First Success (TTFS) (Documentation):**
  Measures the average time it takes a developer to complete
  a primary goal (e.g., first API call) after starting the
  quickstart guide. This matters because it is the ultimate
  measure of a doc's quality and clarity, showing how fast the
  docs accelerate developer activation.

- **Search-to-No-Ticket Ratio (Documentation):**
  Measures the ratio of documentation searches that
  do not result in a related support ticket within a
  short period. This matters because it proves the
  documentation is a successful support cost deflector by
  allowing developers to self-serve their answers.

- **Internal Search Success Rate (Documentation):**
  Measures the rate at which internal documentation
  searches yield a click-through to a relevant page (versus
  "No Results Found"). This matters because it identifies
  crucial content gaps or discoverability issues in your
  information architecture.

- **"Edit/Suggest" Click-Throughs (Documentation):**
  Measures the number of times users click a button
  to suggest a correction or contribution to the docs
  (e.g., on GitHub). This matters because it measures
  the community's willingness to contribute to content
  quality, indicating high engagement and ownership.

- **Satisfaction/Sentiment (Documentation):** Measures direct feedback via "Was this helpful?" widgets or surveys, often resulting in a Documentation Satisfaction Score (DSAT). This matters because it provides fast, contextual feedback on the helpfulness of individual pages, enabling continuous, granular improvement.

- **Repo Forks/Code Usage (Libraries/SDK):** Measures the number of unique developer projects that successfully call a core function of the SDK in a given period. This matters because it is the true measure of active integration and sustained usage, moving beyond vanity metrics like raw download counts.

- **Likes or Stars (Libraries/SDK):** Measures the volume of likes, stars, or similar endorsements on the SDK's repository (e.g., GitHub Stars). This matters because it measures reputation and community endorsement; developers often use this as a proxy for the SDK's quality and maintenance health.

- **API Call Volume (Libraries/SDK):** Measures the volume of API calls made specifically through the SDK compared to calls made directly via HTTP. This matters because it proves the SDK is fulfilling its role as the preferred, low-friction integration mechanism (good DevEx).

- **Quality Contribution Volume (Ambassador Programs):** Measures the total volume of high-value external content (blog posts, tutorials, open-source PRs) created by Ambassadors. This matters because it quantifies the program's ability to amplify your content strategy and scale technical expertise outside the core team.

- **Geographic/Language Reach (Ambassador Programs):**
Measures the number of unique markets (countries,
languages) where Ambassadors are actively hosting events
or publishing content. This matters because it proves the
program is achieving global scaling and reaching segments
that the core team cannot easily access.

- **Ambassador Retention Rate (Ambassador
Programs):** Measures the percentage of Ambassadors
who remain active in the program over a set period
(e.g., year-over-year). This matters because it measures
the value and satisfaction of the program itself, as low
churn indicates effective incentives and support.

- **Community Deflection Rate (Ambassador-Driven)
(Ambassador Programs):** Measures the percentage
of community support questions (Discord, Slack)
answered correctly by an Ambassador instead of a
core team member. This matters because it proves
the program creates a scalable, peer-to-peer support
network, saving internal staff time and resources.

- **Traffic/Views (Podcasts):** Measures total number of
downloads or streams for the episode. This matters
because it measures overall awareness and listenership
volume, providing a baseline reach number.

- **Listener-to-Conversion Rate (Podcasts):** Measures
the percentage of listeners who use a podcast-specific
URL or code to complete a high-value action (signup,
SDK download, community join). This matters because
it directly links the passive audio consumption to active
product adoption and proves the podcast is a viable
DevRel channel.

- **Completion Rate (per episode) (Podcasts):** Measures the percentage of the audience who listen to the entire episode. This matters because a consistently high rate (e.g., >80% for long-form) proves the technical discussion is highly relevant and captivating to the audience.

- **Traffic (Videos):** Measures total video views. This matters because it measures the overall reach and visibility of the content on YouTube and external searches.

- **Average Video Percentage Viewed (Videos):** Measures the average percentage of the video length watched by a viewer. This matters because it proves the video's content and pacing are effective at **holding the developer's attention** through technical explanations.

- **CTA Conversion Rate (Videos):** Measures the CTR on links in the description, pinned comment, or end screen, pointing to documentation or signup. This matters because it measures the video's ability to drive traffic to your owned properties, moving viewers closer to activation.

- **Relative Audience Retention (Videos):** Measures where viewer drop-offs occur on the video timeline compared to other videos. This matters because it pinpoints exact moments of friction (e.g., a complex setup step, a confusing explanation) that need to be addressed in the content or product.

- **Subscriber Growth (Newsletter):** Measures the change in the total number of subscribers over a set period. This matters because it measures the effectiveness of your acquisition efforts and the **overall market demand** for your communication.

- **Open Rate (Newsletter):** Measures the percentage of recipients who open the email. This matters because it measures the effectiveness of the subject line and the sender reputation in getting the attention of a busy developer.

- **Click-Through Rate (CTR) (Newsletter):** Measures the percentage of recipients who click any link in the email. This matters because it measures the newsletter's relevance and value; a high CTR proves the content is driving action.

- **List Churn Rate (Newsletter):** Measures the percentage of subscribers who unsubscribe from the list after each send. This matters because a low churn rate indicates the content remains highly **valuable and relevant** over time, sustaining long-term interest.

- **CTA Conversion Rate (Newsletter):** Measures the CTR for a specific, high-priority link or CTA in the newsletter (e.g., "Install New SDK"). This matters because it measures how effectively the newsletter drives a single, measurable DevRel priority.

- **Engagement or Replies (Social Media):** Measures the total volume of comments, replies, and mentions on your posts. This matters because replies often indicate high technical interest and willingness to engage with the product, measuring the quality and depth of the conversation.

- **Community Join Rate (Social Media):** Measures the number of developers who click a social link to join your Discord, Slack, or forum. This matters because it proves the channel is transitioning developers from passive followers to active members of your owned community.

- **Traffic/Likes/Shares/Views (Social Media):** Measures the raw volume of traffic directed to your site, along with surface-level social interactions. This matters because it provides a baseline for **reach and awareness**, but should be contextualized against conversion metrics.

- **CTA Conversion Rate (Social Media):** Measures the CTR on a link in the social post pointing to documentation, GitHub, or a signup page. This matters because it measures how well social content drives measurable action toward high-value destinations.

- **Exam Pass Rate (Training or Certification Programs):** Measures the percentage of candidates who pass the final certification exam. This matters because it measures the effectiveness of the curriculum and ensures the program is upholding the required standard of skill.

- **Student Satisfaction Score (Training or Certification Programs):** Measures a direct survey rating on the training material, platform experience, and perceived value immediately after completion. This matters because it provides fast feedback to improve the training experience and increase word-of-mouth promotion.

- **Completion Rate (Training or Certification Programs):** Measures the percentage of registered students who successfully finish the entire course modules or curriculum. This matters because a high rate proves the course is well-structured and engaging, minimizing drop-off due to friction or difficulty.

- **Feedback Volume (Event Sponsorships):** Measures the number of unique, high-priority bug reports, feature requests, or product insights gathered from developer conversations at the event. This matters because it proves the sponsorship is a vital channel for gathering product intelligence that influences the roadmap.

- **Competitive Intelligence Gained (Event Sponsorships):** Measures the volume of new information gathered about competitors' products, messaging, or pricing through developer conversations. This matters because it provides strategic information that informs marketing and product positioning after the event.

- **Follow-Up Engagement Rate (Event Sponsorships):** Measures the percentage of qualified leads from the event who engage with the first piece of post-event follow-up content (e.g., opening a personalized email). This matters because it tests the quality of the initial interaction and the effectiveness of your lead-nurturing workflow.

Index

L. Ikechukwu, *A Friendly Guide to Developer Advocacy*, Friendly Guides to Technology, https://doi.org/10.1007/979-8-8688-2462-3

D

L

M

N

O

U

GPSR Compliance
The European Union's (EU) General Product Safety Regulation (GPSR) is a set
of rules that requires consumer products to be safe and our obligations to
ensure this.

If you have any concerns about our products, you can contact us on

ProductSafety@springernature.com

In case Publisher is established outside the EU, the EU authorized
representative is:

Springer Nature Customer Service Center GmbH
Europaplatz 3
69115 Heidelberg, Germany